CHECKING IRAN'S NUCLEAR AMBITIONS

Edited by

Henry Sokolski
Patrick Clawson

University Press of the Pacific
Honolulu, Hawaii

Checking Iran's Nuclear Ambitions

Edited by
Henry Sokolski
Patrick Clawson

ISBN: 1-4102-1763-9

Reprinted from the 2004 edition

University Press of the Pacific
Honolulu, Hawaii
http://www.universitypressofthepacific.com

CONTENTS

PREFACE

In his introduction to the September 2002 National Security Strategy of the United States, President George W. Bush wrote, "The gravest danger our Nation faces lies at the crossroads of radicalism and technology. Our enemies have openly declared that they are seeking weapons of mass destruction (WMD), and evidence indicates that they are doing so with determination. . . . Terrorists are organized to penetrate open societies and to turn the power of modern technologies against us."

Iran is the poster-child for the nexus of terrorism and WMD. It is the world's foremost state-sponsor of terrorism, as well as one of the countries most actively pursuing nuclear weapons. Washington is vigilant about Iran's support for a network of Islamist terrorist organizations and persistent in pressing Iran to end its financial, political, material, and operational support to them. At the same time, the United States has to come up with effective strategies to ensure that Iran does not acquire nuclear weapons. Were Iran to acquire nuclear weapons, there is a grave risk it would be tempted to provide them to terrorists. After all, mass casualty terrorism done by proxies has worked well for Iran to date. Iranian assistance to the terrorists who blew up the U.S. and French barracks in Beirut in 1983 was a grand strategic success, forcing the United States, and for a while France, out of Lebanon while not bringing any retaliation down on Iran. Similarly, the 1996 bombing of the Khobar Towers barracks in Saudi Arabia caused the Saudis to make a strategic reconciliation, and, once again, Iran faced no retaliation.

The fear about what Iran might do with nuclear weapons is fed by the concern that Tehran has no clear reason to be pursuing nuclear weapons. The strategic rationale for Iran's nuclear program is by no means obvious. Unlike proliferators such as Israel or Pakistan, Iran faces no historic enemy who would welcome an opportunity to wipe the state off the face of the earth. Iran is encircled by troubled neighbors, but nuclear weapons do nothing to help counter the threats that could come from state collapse in Afghanistan, Pakistan, Iraq, or Azerbaijan. Instead, Iranian acquisition of nuclear

v

arms could set off a chain reaction—increased U.S. assets directed against Iran, active Israeli planning for Iran contingencies, and quite possibly nuclear proliferation by Iranian neighbors such as Saudi Arabia and Turkey—which would leave Iran worse off than if it had never developed nuclear arms. Instead of starting an arms race that it is certain to lose, Iran would be much better off strategically if it pressed for agreements to limit arms throughout the Gulf: to restrict the size of the new Iraqi army, to freeze and reduce the size of the Arab Gulf monarchies' militaries, and to phase down the size of the U.S. force in the area. However, Iran's leaders seem remarkably impervious to careful strategic thinking about international security; put another way, perhaps they are more driven by considerations of national prestige or domestic politics.

Hopefully European and American leaders will agree on how to proceed about Iran's nuclear program. To date, European leaders seem to concentrate on significant incentives ("bigger carrots") for responsible behavior to the near exclusion of threatening painful, punitive measures ("bigger sticks") for continued irresponsible behavior, while Americans do the reverse. It would be progress if each side more openly acknowledged that the most promising approach combines both carrots and sticks, and if each side more bluntly stated that it was prepared to consider using both instruments. That said, it is at least possible that, in the end, Europe will take the lead in offering Iran incentives while the United States takes the lead in threatening punitive measures.

Achieving trans-Atlantic consensus on how to respond to Iran's nuclear program will be difficult. This is a remarkably bad time for the international community to face the Iran nuclear problem, because the tensions about the Iraq WMD issue still poison relations and weaken U.S. ability to respond. Nevertheless, Iran's nuclear program poses a stark challenge to the international nonproliferation regime. The intelligence about the Iran threat is coming from a United Nations agency—namely, the International Atomic Energy Agency (IAEA)—and there is no doubt that Iran is developing worrisome capabilities. If the world community led by Western countries is unable to prevent Iranian proliferation, then it is unclear that there is much meaning to global nonproliferation norms.

Iran's nuclear program raises stark shortcomings with the global nonproliferation norms. The basic deal behind the Treaty on the Non-Proliferation of Nuclear Weapons (NPT) is that countries are allowed to acquire a wide range of troubling capabilities in return for being open and transparent. The NPT gives Iran every right to have a full closed fuel cycle, with large uranium enrichment facilities and a reprocessing plant that can extract substantial amounts of plutonium—capabilities which would permit Iran at any time to rapidly "break out" of the NPT, building a considerable number of nuclear weapons in a short time. Had Iran been fully transparent about its nuclear activities, then even if Iran had gone so far as to operate a full closed fuel cycle, the international community would have been split deeply about how to react. It is fortunate indeed that Iran decided to cheat on its NPT obligations by hiding some of what is doing, because that has made much easier the construction of an international consensus that Iran's nuclear program is troubling. But the experience with Iran should lead to reflection about whether the basic NPT deal needs to be revisited.

PATRICK CLAWSON
Deputy Director
Washington Institute for
Near East Policy

INTRODUCTION

Henry Sokolski

Considering the latest Iranian nuclear developments, one might question whether a study now on how best to restrain Tehran is simply one that's come too late. To be sure, estimates vary as to when Iran could build its first bomb. Some believe Tehran could do it before the end of 2005; others think Iran would only be able to do so by the end of the decade. In either case, though, the die seems cast: If Iran wants, it has all that it needs eventually to build a bomb on its own. Certainly, trying to deny Iran further nuclear technology in the hopes that this will prevent it from getting nuclear weapons is no longer a credible strategy.

The questions this edited volume addresses are whether or not any strategy can prevent Iran from going nuclear, what the proper goals of such a strategy might be (deterring use, keeping Tehran from deploying weapons, getting it to dismantle its nuclear program, etc.), and what other nonproliferation goals ought to be attempted (including trying to dissuade other nations from following Iran's example). The answers this volume offers are: 1) in the long-run Iran will gain little from going nuclear, and 2) much can be gained by enforcing the nonproliferation rules Iran agreed to and spelling out the costs to Iran of its continuing acquisition of nuclear weapons-related capabilities.

The book's seven chapters were commissioned as the first of a two-part Nonproliferation Policy Education Center (NPEC) project on Iran supported by the Smith Richardson Foundation and the Office of Net Assessment within the Department of Defense. The project's interim conclusions and policy recommendations are contained in this book's first chapter, "Checking Iran's Nuclear Ambitions." The key point made here is that whatever is done to keep Iran from proceeding with its nuclear program should be done with a eye toward deterring other states, including Iran's neighbors, from following Tehran's example of using the NPT and the International Atomic Energy Agency (IAEA) to get within weeks of having a large arsenal of nuclear weapons. The details of just how Iran has been able to do this are spelled out in the book's second chapter, "Iran's 'Legal' Paths to the Bomb," by former U.S. Nuclear Regulatory Commissioner Victor Gilinsky. In this chapter, Mr. Gilinsky details how Iran can use Bushehr and its "civilian" uranium enrichment program to come within weeks of having dozens of bombs even while being intrusively inspected by the IAEA.

Would Iran ever actually deploy nuclear weapons though? Much depends on one's read of just how long-lived and truculent the current regime is. These issues are taken up in the volume's next two chapters. In "Iran's Internal Struggles," Genieve Abdo, an internationally recognized observer of Iranian politics, argues that the revolutionary government is unlikely to be overthrown anytime soon and that it will persist in its hostile foreign policies. Rob Sobhani, a leading American-Iranian commentator, however, argues that with sufficient U.S. support of the right sort, the current government in Iran could give way to a far more liberal and peaceable regime. But what is the "right" kind of support? Abbas William Samii, Radio Free Europe's Iranian broadcast analyst, explores this question in chapter 5, "Winning Iranian Hearts and Minds." Although Mr. Samii does not rule out speedy regime change, he warns that it is not likely and that for that reason, the United States needs to have a long-term outreach program that will encourage a more favorable opinion of the United States among the general Iranian population.

This, then, raises the question of timing. If favorable regime change may not come before Iran acquires nuclear weapons or the ability to quickly acquire them, what other course of action might the United States and its allies take to influence Iranian decisionmakers? One course would be to try to cut Iran a deal. As former U.S. National Security Council staffer and Nixon Center Middle East expert Geoffrey Kemp explains in chapter 6, the history of such efforts has been mixed. Mr. Kemp, though, argues that circumstances now might actually be ripe for fruitful negotiations. And what if they are not? In the book's final chapter, Michael Eisenstadt, the Washington Institute's Gulf security analyst, raises the veil on what might be the last resort--military action. In his chapter, "The Challenges of U.S. Preventive Military Action," Mr. Eisenstadt details the various risks associated with both overt and covert military attacks against Iran's nuclear program.

None of the most popular policy options, in short, are sure bets; all are fraught with dangers. This is why it is critical to make sure that Iran at least understands that it will not be rewarded or given a pass on its pursuit of worrisome nuclear activities. In the first instance this means that the United States and its allies must make full use of existing restraints against nuclear weapons proliferation-- the IAEA and the NPT--to make sure Iran does not become a model of how to exploit the rules, but rather an example of what happens to states that bend or flaunt them. Beyond this, the United States and its allies must make clear what Iran can expect if it continues its nuclear power program--even if within the legal letter of the IAEA Statute--and how much better Iran's future would be if it terminated its program and cut its ties to terrorists, who might otherwise gain access to the nuclear know-how Iran has already mastered.

In the end, of course, diplomacy is meaningless unless it is backed by the prospect of force. Cooperative military planning, creating new security arrangements, covert military actions, defense cooperation and transfers that are aimed at limiting the harm Iran's nuclear activities might otherwise pose will all soon become urgent matters. What specifically needs to be done will be more fully detailed upon completion of this project's second phase, later in 2004.

CHAPTER 1

CHECKING IRAN'S NUCLEAR AMBITIONS: REPORT RECOMMENDATIONS

Nonproliferation Policy Education Center Project on Iran

This report is based on commissioned research and commentary of over 30 of the nation's leading experts on Iran and nuclear proliferation. It was over a year in the making. Unlike most analyses, which have focused solely on the immediate worry of Iran going nuclear, it sees Iran's nuclear program as a persistent danger and catalyst for other states to acquire nuclear weapons options of their own. These nuclear programs along with Iran's would confront the United States and its allies with intolerable long-term security dangers. The report supports neither overt military action against Iran's nuclear facilities nor trying to cut a deal with Iran not to make nuclear weapons. Instead, it makes three recommendations, none of which U.S. or allied officials have yet fully adopted:

1. *Challenge Iran's Non-Proliferation Treaty (NPT) noncompliance as being decisive to the future of nuclear nonproliferation.* If Iran succeeds in coming within weeks of being able to breakout of the NPT and quickly acquire nuclear weapons, it will demonstrate to the world (and every other nation that might want nuclear weapons) how any state can use the NPT to get the bombmaking capabilities it wants. Unlike what happened with Iraq or North Korea, then, the United States and other like-minded nations need to enforce and amplify the NPT to curb Iran *before* it acquires more than a bomb's worth of separated plutonium or highly enriched uranium (HEU). Toward this end, the International Atomic Energy Agency (IAEA) should be urged to follow the requirements of its charter and at least file an interim report to the United Nations Security Council (UNSC) about the known technical IAEA violations Iran has itself admitted to, and highlight concerns the IAEA still has about additional Iranian

1

weapons-related activities relating to the trace quantities of HEU that the IAEA has found. In addition, this report should:

- insist that Iran uphold the freeze on its uranium enrichment and processing activities that it agreed to October 21 with Germany, France, and the United Kingdom;

- establish a reasonable schedule for clarifying the origin of the trace amounts of the bomb usable HEU the IAEA has found;

- call on all nations to temporarily suspend any further nuclear cooperation with Iran until the IAEA can clarify this matter and establish whether or not Iran has come into full compliance with the NPT; and,

- ask the permanent five members of the UNSC (P-5) to agree to how they would act upon receipt of an IAEA report that found a member to be not clearly in full compliance with either its IAEA safeguards agreement or the NPT.

Among the country-neutral resolutions that the P-5 should consider and urge the UNSC to adopt while the IAEA is evaluating the evidence concerning Iran's compliance status are:

- authorizing UN members to interdict the imports of any technology, material, or equipment relevant to the development of nuclear weapons or their means of delivery to any nation that the IAEA had formally identified as no longer being clearly in full compliance with its NPT obligations;

- banning any peaceful nuclear cooperation with such states the IAEA has identified until the IAEA confirms its full compliance with the NPT;

- prohibiting NPT members from withdrawing from the treaty (i.e., requiring the imposition of all the obligations of the NPT on all NPT members whether they have been identified by the IAEA or not) unless or until they first surrender all of the nuclear capabilities they previously gained while a member of the treaty;

- authorizing the imposition of UN and UN member state economic penalties against states the IAEA has identified as no longer clearly being in full compliance with their NPT obligations on a progressive basis, starting with small measures (e.g., a ban on loans from international financial institutions) and escalating to harsher measures; and,

- creating a P-5 NPT secretariat to see to it that above measures are actually implemented.

The aim of these resolutions (and their development, which would take several months) would be three-fold. First, their development and adoption should help deter further violation of the NPT by Iran and spell out what action the UNSC would take when the IAEA finally determines Iran's compliance status. Second, they (and their country-neutral character) should help deter Iran's neighbors, or other nations, who might otherwise be tempted to hedge their security bets by acquiring a nuclear weapons option of their own. Third, they should help give the Russians and the Europeans additional justification for withholding preferential trade and nuclear cooperation from Iran if it persists in developing a nuclear weapons option.

Finally, for reasons detailed later in this report, it is clear from the evidence the IAEA has found already that the agency ultimately will have to conclude that Iran is no longer clearly in full compliance with its NPT obligations, i.e., that Iran is in violation. This, in turn, should trigger the sanction responses detailed above.

2. *Encourage Iranians to debate the merits of their nuclear power program and support of terrorism.* The IAEA demands made of Iran at its last board of governors' meeting on September 12, 2003, prompted a limited debate. Iranian officials, however, were not pressed very hard. Although some hardliners still object to Iran making any concessions, no official has yet conceded

that Tehran should give up its enrichment or power reactor programs. Nor has any Iranian official argued that Iran can do more than it already has to explain the mysterious HEU traces IAEA inspectors found. A key reason why more debate has not been generated in Iran about Tehran's nuclear policies is that few in the United States or Europe have insisted that Iran do much more than minimally satisfy the IAEA. This must change.

First, the more Iranians are pressed on their nuclear policies and continued support of terrorism, the more likely it is that the current government will make additional needed concessions. Second, and more important, the more Iran is pressed on these issues, the more likely it is that the internal debate it produces in Iran will itself foster greater firmness within the international community to press on these matters. This, in turn, will be critical to warn off other states from ever trying to emulate Iran's example. Of course, those that want to work with the revolutionary government in Iran claim that is what they are trying to accomplish by offering to cut Tehran a deal—i.e., to give it benefits up front in exchange for promises of better Iranian behavior later. The history of the last 2 decades of such deal making, however, is a story of time invested with little to show in return. In the case of deal making over Iran's nuclear program, the time lost, moreover, will only bring Iran closer to acquiring bombs. Instead of taking this approach, then, the United States and its allies should make it clear to Iranians what they can expect the costs and benefits will be to their country of pursing alternative nuclear foreign policies. Specifically, after the P-5 considers the country-neutral proliferation-related resolutions noted above, and the IAEA and the UNSC sanction Iran, the United States and its friends should highlight the prospect of Iran having to engage in a competition against most of its neighbors and the world and contrast this with the benefits Iran could expect to receive if it relinquished its nuclear power program and cut its ties with terrorist organizations. Tehran should be told that if it fails to follow up its latest October 21, 2003, pledge to suspend its enrichment of uranium with verifiable moves to dismantle its nuclear power program, it will risk being further isolated economically, diplomatically, and militarily. Conversely, the major powers should make it clear that Iran can expect to receive security guarantees, an end to U.S. sanctions, and access to high technology and international capital markets if Iran dismantles all of its nuclear power-related facilities (i.e., all but its small research reactor facilities) and ends its support of terrorist organizations. The deadlines for Tehran taking these remedial actions should be early and clear—i.e., well before Iran could possibly acquire its first bomb—within 24 months or less. At the same time and to assure this explanation has credibility among Iranian reformers, the United States should launch additional long-term initiatives to undermine the revolutionary government's efforts to demonize America. These initiatives should include more creative forms of outreach as well as direct forms of relief such as increased disaster relief and public health assistance.

3. *If Iran continues to pursue worrisome nuclear activities, ramp up U.S. and allied military regional capabilities both to neutralize the Iranian threat and forestall further proliferation.* The United States and the military coalition in Iraq already must guarantee Iraq's security against a potentially hostile Iran. The United States and its key allies are also committed to interdicting commerce in nuclear weapons-related items to trouble states like Iran under the Proliferation Security Initiative. Beyond this, the United States and its key allies ought to consult with the Gulf Coordination Council states, Jordan, Turkey, Israel, and Egypt about what these nations' military plans are for coping with a militant, nuclear (or near-nuclear) Iran. Plans should be prepared now on how additional military cooperation (including intelligence sharing, missile defense cooperation, joint training, base sharing agreements, etc.) might best counter the threat and what new security arrangements, if any, would be appropriate. Details on these issues will be developed as a part of the Nonproliferation Policy Education Center's (NPEC) planned follow on study, which will be completed in 2004.

Principal Assumptions.

Some may see these recommendations as harsh. Given what the IAEA has learned about Iran's nuclear weapons effort, though, the urgency of addressing Iran's possible breakout has clearly increased. Stunned earlier this year by the discovery of several new nuclear production facilities, trace quantities of highly enriched uranium, and Iran's admission to making uranium metal and importing significant quantities of special nuclear materials from China, most experts now believe Iran could get a bomb within 3 to 5 years, while some analysts fear it could do so in 24 months or less. Given the size of Iran's nuclear power-related facilities, completion of its first weapon, moreover, could quickly be followed by the production of scores of weapons. Iran's neighbors—nations that are all historically allied with the United States, including Israel, Saudi Arabia, Turkey, and Egypt—are unlikely to welcome Iran coming so close to acquiring nuclear weapons. The adverse responses they might take include seeking new security ties, acquiring their own nuclear weapons options and relying less on the United States to assure their security.

All of these possibilities highlight America's need to act decisively with its closest friends to dissuade Iran from continuing on its current path and to make sure that no nation emulates Iran's nuclear example. The question is how.

Currently, there are three fashionable proposals to curb Iran's nuclear program, each of which is too uncertain or too self-defeating to effectively address the nuclear threat.

- **Bomb Iran's Known Nuclear Sites**. Iranians fear this. Exercising this option, though, is risky. A "surgical" strike could start a war (Iranian counterstrikes against U.S. forces in Iraq or terrorist strikes elsewhere against the United States and Israel, etc.). Even with the best planning, such a strike would be unlikely to destroy all of Iran's covert weapons efforts or stop its weapons scientists from resuming work. To maximize surprise, the United States (or Israel) would want to attack before securing other nations' support. This, however, could jeopardize international backing to contain Iran afterwards and would likely raise serious doubts about the utility of the NPT and the IAEA—norms that might otherwise help justify such a raid.

- **Change the Regime**. The United States and its allies say they want to promote human rights and pluralistic politics in Iran. Ultimately, this requires regime change (whether by overthrow or major reform). How might this advance nuclear nonproliferation in Iran? Is the regime in Iran likely to change before it acquires a bomb? Would a new government end the nuclear program (or surrender any bomb materials it might have produced)? How (if at all) could promoting such a change stigmatize Iran as an NPT violator to discourage would be bombmakers from following suit? The answers to these questions remain unclear.

- **Cut a Deal**. Many officials in Europe, Asia, Russia, and China favor cutting a deal with Tehran. They would like to see the understanding the United Kingdom, France, and Germany reached with Iran on October 21, 2003, as the first step toward a larger deal. The logic of this approach is to give Iran what it wants—U.S. recognition, lifting of U.S. sanctions, U.S. security guarantees and, in time, withdrawal of U.S. military forces in the Gulf and access to advanced technology and Western markets— for what we want—an end to Iran's dangerous nuclear activities, a cut-off of support of terrorist organizations, and adherence to agreed human rights strictures. But how long would it take to conclude such a deal? How could one prevent Iran from stringing the United States and its allies along until it acquired all it needed to breakout with a nuclear arsenal? Given what Iran could do covertly and the vast amounts of plutonium its power reactors would be producing, how likely is any inspection, including the IAEA's new 1992+3 inspection protocol, to detect covert enrichment or reprocessing activities early enough to prevent Iran's speedy completion of a bomb? Could the current government, which has already cheated on the NPT, be trusted to deliver on its promises? How could any deal be cut without it looking like a reward for Iran skirting the NPT? Would such a deal with the hard-line government undercut pro-American democratic reformers by suggesting that America's real interest is geo-strategic realpolitik rather than support for liberalization? How could a deal be squared with the Bush administration's declaration that past deals with Middle East autocrats fed anti-Americanism and terrorism and that it is now in U.S. strategic interests to transform the Middle East?

Considering only these options, the outlook for halting Iran's program seems grim. Yet, if one views the current nuclear crisis as part of a larger, long-term, security competition, the United States and its friends have clear advantages that would allow them to take approaches different from the those described above. In a year-long series of NPEC workshops, 30 regional experts, in fact, identified three enduring weaknesses of the current Iranian regime that could be exploited:

- **It is enormously unpopular.** Recent student demonstrations and the consequent government crack down (with thousands of arrests) are indicative of how 70 percent of the population (now under age 30 with no memory of the 1979 revolution) feels. The government's fear of popular resistance forces it to fractionate and repress a variety of government bodies to guard against significant political reform. It also requires it to maintain an external threat to sustain domestic control. As a result, Iranian officials tend to demonize the United States and Israel and obsess about what Iran's immediate neighbors might do. This last point has immediate implications for any negotiated deal over Iran's nuclear program. When members of Iran's Expediency Council met in Geneva with the co-chairmen of this project, they had difficulty believing the United States and its allies would reverse their hostility toward Iran if Iran cut off its ties to terrorist organizations, promoted human rights, and terminated its nuclear program. Instead, they wanted the United States to agree to a list of demands before Iran acted.

- **It is strategically lonely.** Iran lacks friends and does not work well with others. Despite its most recent agreement to suspend

8

its uranium enrichment activities (for how long, is still unclear), it still is at odds with the European Union (EU) over human rights; the IAEA for dodging agency resolutions that it come totally clean on its nuclear past; and the United States and most of the world for harboring and supporting terrorists—now including Al Qaeda agents—who are all too willing to use any means (including chemical, biological, or nuclear devices) to attack Israel, Europe, and the United States. Given its loneliness, Tehran is particularly anxious to avoid being brought before the UN. Meanwhile, locally, Iran is suspicious of nearly all of its neighbors and is still quite frightened of being attacked or subverted by the United States or Israel. This, in turn, encourages it to turn inward. The end result is that the country that Iran now has the closest military cooperation with—North Korea—is itself on the outs. As for its closest diplomatic allies—Russia and China—these states' help is triggered less by Iran's needs than a desire to oppose the United States.

- **It is desperate for Western help**. The flip-side of Iran's strategic loneliness is its overweening sense of self-importance. Iranian officials believe that Iran should be the most powerful and richest state in the region and cannot understand why it is not. Meanwhile, Iran's high level of corruption and state interference in the economy has wrecked the economy and produced a domestic unemployment rate of over 25 percent: To deal with this, Iran must let over 200,000 of its young people emigrate annually to the West to find work. As Iranian officials see it, the only way to reverse these trends is to get full access to advanced Western technology, Western financial assets, and America's enormous export market.

What is interesting about these weaknesses is how they feed one another: The more strategically lonely Iran gets, the more desperate it is for Western help; the more unpopular its government becomes, the more it blames outside forces for its shortcomings. This, in turn, only makes it more strategically isolated. There was considerable debate among the workshop participants about how long the current regime might last and what it would take to bring it down—some thinking it was fragile, most thinking that it would go on for many years. But, in the end, all thought Iran would eventually give way to some more moderate form of rule.

Given the uncertainly regarding the revolutionary government's longevity, the question arises as to how the United States and its friends should proceed against Iran's nuclear program, which is progressing at a rapid rate. If the objective is to try to terminate the program immediately, the shortcomings of the three most popular options already noted come into play. If, on the other hand, the objective is to keep Iran from making or deploying nuclear weapons and to make sure Iran does not become a model for other would be bombmakers to follow, then the United States and its friends can exploit the Revolutionary government's enduring weaknesses. With proper care, the United States and its allies could even see Iran's current government give way to a less hostile regime. These long-term aims were the ones the working group believed were the ones most worthy of U.S. and allied effort and would require timely application of one or more of America's and its allies' strengths. These include:

- **Power to lead and maintain military alliances.** In the last 16 years, the United States has operated alone or in concert effectively against Iran, Iraq and Afghanistan. More importantly, after toppling Saddam and the Taliban, the United States and its friends have made it clear that they will be backing Iraq's and Afghanistan's security, and in all probability operating out of Iraq and Afghanistan for the next decade or more. In addition, the United States has friendly military relations with the U.K., Spain, Poland, Japan, most of the EU, Pakistan, Israel, Egypt, Kuwait, Turkey, Jordan, and most of the Gulf Cooperation Council. It also has close ties with several nations that have extensive experience operating covertly against a variety of Middle Eastern nations.

- **Ability to apply economic leverage.** The United States, the EU, and Japan have all been on record as opposing Iran's nuclear weapons activities. All have backed the IAEA's efforts to get Iran to come clean on its previously undeclared nuclear activities.

Japan has held back from investing billions for oil development in Iran. The EU, meanwhile, has put off extending a major trade protocol with Iran until and unless it makes its nuclear program more transparent, improves its human rights record, and ends its ties with terrorist organizations. Germany, France, and Great Britain indicated in their October 21 understanding that Iran "could expect easier access to modern technology and supplies in a wide range of areas," but only if it suspends its enrichment and processing activities and is able to convince the IAEA that its nuclear activities are entirely peaceful. Also, the United States, which constitutes Iran's largest potential export market, could expand trade with Tehran significantly, if it chose to do so. To date, Washington has cut off private U.S. investment in Iran and has frozen Iranian overseas assets which Iran erroneously believes amount to billions of dollars.

- **Attractive alternative political and social culture.** The United States and Europe are culturally attractive to a majority of Iranian citizens. Many have visited and studied in the West and continue to do so. More have listened to or seen Western popular music, television, or movies. Western democracy is also seen as an attractive political alternative. The current government encourages some expressions of popular will and is quite sensitive about its lack of popularity for this reason. Recently, the government actually paid Cuba to jam alternative Iranian broadcasting from Los Angeles for fear of its seditious influence. Precisely because the government paints the United States as the Great Satan, embracing aspects of U.S. and Western culture is seen by Iranians as a way to resist.

Competitive Strategies.

Keeping these strengths in mind, participants in NPEC's workshops suggested that the United States and its friends approach curbing Iran's nuclear ambitions as part of a larger, more general competition whose aims would include:

- demonstrating U.S. and allied support for the welfare of common Iranians. This effort should be geared to help undermine the Revolutionary government's efforts to portray the United States and its friends as security threats that warrant repressive domestic rule;

- making it clear to Iran and its neighbors (i.e., Saudi Arabia, Egypt, Syria, and Turkey) that following Iran's nuclear example or violating the NPT is a poor way to hedge their own security bets, and that NPT and IAEA requirements are firm and will be in enforced.

- showing America's allies who believe a quick deal with Iran is possible and desirable that any sound understanding—one with clear, worthwhile goals, and deadlines—is something that the current regime is incapable of delivering on until and unless the government undergoes major change.

- alerting Iran that any further progress on its "civilian" nuclear power program risks isolating it further and increasing the military risks it otherwise would not have to run.

- creating a P-5 NPT secretariat to see to it that above measures are actually implemented.

To achieve these larger goals, the group concluded that the United States and its friends should pursue a series at least three separate but related competitive strategies. These strategies' ultimate aim would be to deter and delay Iran and its neighbors from developing or deploying nuclear weapons, keep America's allies united in opposing the current regime's most threatening activities, and increase pressures on the current regime either to change or to give way to a less hostile one that would be less wedded to having nuclear weapons:

1. Challenge Iran's NPT noncompliance as being decisive to the future of nuclear nonproliferation. The United States has done well to get the IAEA Board of Governors (including Russia) to demand that

Iran freeze its enrichment and possible reprocessing facilities, allow more intrusive inspections, and clarify its past nuclear activities. Firmness on these points prompted Iran to agree to accede to these demands in an understanding reached with Germany, France, and the United Kingdom on October 21, 2003. Senior Iranian officials made it very clear that under no circumstances could their country succeed if the matter of their nuclear activities were characterized as being illegal and were referred to the UN for action. An immediate danger now that Tehran has said it would comply with the IAEA's September 12 demands, however, is that the United States or its allies might settle for only partial delivery on Iran's pledges. Given growing evidence that Iran is developing a nuclear weapons option, such weakness would not only give Iran a pass to pursue its nuclear ambitions, but encourage other nuclear weapons aspirants (starting with Iran's neighbors) to follow in Tehran's footsteps. This later prospect is at least as worrisome as the first. It will likely take the IAEA some months to make sense of the Iranian documents and nuclear equipment it is now examining in its effort to determine Iran's NPT compliance status. During this period, the IAEA should call for a temporary suspension of all nuclear cooperation with Iran. Ultimately, however, the IAEA will have little choice but to find Iran either to be in violation or not clearly in full compliance and this, in turn, should prompt sanctions. Indeed, doing anything less would seriously jeopardize the IAEA's credibility and that of the NPT. The reasons why already are plain:

- Iran has already admitted to violating its safeguards agreement with the IAEA by not properly alerting the IAEA about its importation of uranium and conversion of uranium into metal.

- The IAEA's own statute stipulates that the agency must report all safeguards violations to the UNSC. As such, not to report would be to have the IAEA punt on its own procedures and suggest that the IAEA can be duped or bullied.

- Although the IAEA set October 31, 2003 as the deadline for Iran to explain the trace amounts of HEU the IAEA found, Iranian officials claim that they will never be able to fully resolve this mystery except to claim that the centrifuge equipment they imported was "contaminated" and that the brokers that sold this equipment can't say where they bought this equipment from.

- HEU is directly usable to make kiloton-yield weapons.

- There is good reason to believe that this equipment came by way of Pakistan's or Russia's nuclear weapons program (which goes to Iran's intent to build weapons in violation of Article II of the NPT, a key provision that prohibits non-weapons state members from seeking or receiving "any assistance in the manufacture of nuclear weapons"). On this last point, Iranian officials insist that the burden of proof that it is in violation is on the IAEA. Yet, just the reverse is the case: Once a state is found in possession of undeclared special nuclear materials, the burden is on it to explain how it could possess such material without being found in violation of the NPT.

- If Iran did enrich uranium to make HEU, it would have violated its IAEA safeguards agreement since it would have failed to notify the IAEA of the introduction of special nuclear material into an undeclared enrichment facility.

- If the IAEA fails to report these points to the UNSC as the IAEA's charter requires, it will appear weak and only encourage more Iranian welshing (e.g., Iranian officials' recent announcement that it is "studying" how it could possibly suspend its enrichment activity).

- Finally, unless an IAEA violations finding is in prospect (or its functional equivalent—i.e., an IAEA finding that it cannot find Iran to be in full compliance), any state could simply follow Iran's example and violate the NPT or IAEA in the expectation that the IAEA would give them a similar pass.

In addition to these points, members of the IAEA's board of governors should reflect on IAEA director general el Baradei's own recent public warnings that were prominently featured in the

14

October 18, 2003, edition of *The Economist*. In a detailed column that he authored, the director general spoke out about the limitations of IAEA inspections. There is no monitoring effort, he explained, not even the additional protocol the IAEA is asking Iran to implement, that can prevent nations from acquiring nuclear weapons so long as they are allowed to have enrichment, reprocessing, and power reactor programs. NPEC-commissioned research corroborates these points. If Iran uses natural uranium, it could make its first bomb in 36 months or less. In the case of using light water reactor fresh fuel as enrichment feed, the time lines would be much shorter—under selected scenarios, a matter of days or weeks. Once Iran's light water power reactor is up and running, the time lines for it making plutonium for bombs are also short. The Russians announced in the fall of 2003 that they intend to slip the completion date of the reactor another 2 years. It remains to be seen if the Russians stick to this schedule. Russia has also proposed to take back any spent fuel generated from Bushehr. In any case, 12-15 months after the reactor goes into operation, it will contain roughly 60 bombs' worth of near weapons-grade plutonium. With only modest investment, Iran could easily build a reprocessing plant covertly at any time in 4 to 6 months in a space 30 feet by 40 feet by 130 feet, using readily accessible technology. With such a facility on the ready, Iran could run the reactor and then tell inspectors and Russians that it wants to examine the spent fuel. This might cause alarm (or not); it would hardly matter. In as little as a week, well before anyone could agree on the facts, much less a clear course of action, Iran could make a bomb's worth of plutonium metal a day.

It is for this reason and because of Iran's past cheating (and its contradictory explanations about the trace quantities of HEU inspectors found), that the IAEA should report to the UNSC even before it completes its analysis of Iranian documents and equipment associated with the agency's discovery of trace quantities of HEU. In this "interim" report, the IAEA should:

- call on all nations to suspend temporarily any further nuclear cooperation with Iran until the IAEA can clarify this matter and establish whether or not Iran has come into full compliance with the NPT;

- insist that Iran uphold the freeze on its uranium enrichment and processing activities that it agreed to October 21, 2003 with Germany, France, and the United Kingdom;

- establish a reasonable schedule for clarifying the origin of the trace amounts of bomb usable highly enriched uranium (HEU) the IAEA has found.

- ask the permanent five members of the UNSC (P-5) to agree to how they would act upon receipt of an IAEA report that found a member not to be clearly in full compliance with either its IAEA safeguards agreement or the NPT.

The filing of this report would be immediately beneficial. At the very least, it would help provide the justification the Russians need to keep from completing Bushehr. This is important. Without Bushehr, Iran lacks any "peaceful" justification for mining, enriching, or reprocessing nuclear materials for power production. Also, without this reactor, Iran would be deprived of the lightly enriched uranium fuel required to complete the two quickest routes to generating a large number of nuclear weapons—weapons usable plutonium from Bushehr's spent fuel or weapons uranium derived from the lightly enriched uranium it could feed into its centrifuge program.

It also could help set a major revitalization of the NPT into motion by getting the P-5 focused on enforcing the NPT. Such an effort is urgently needed since the UNSC has still taken no action on the IAEA's violation report it filed in February 2003 regarding North Korea.

Among the NPT enforcement actions the P-5 ought to consider and adopt are:

- calling on all nations to cooperate in interdicting all nuclear related exports and imports to and from the identified violator until that nation comes back into full compliance with the NPT;

- banning any further peaceful nuclear cooperation with any state the IAEA has determined is not clearly in full compliance with its NPT obligations until such time as the agency validates full adherence;

- insisting that all of the provisions of the NPT continue to apply to states even if they then attempt to withdraw from the NPT until and unless they dismantle or surrender the nuclear goods they have acquired under the NPT;

- authorizing increasingly stiff economic sanctions against states the IAEA identifies as no longer clearly being in full compliance with their NPT obligations starting with the suspension of international financial institutional investments so long as the noncompliant state fails to resolve its violations; and,

- creating a P-5 NPT secretariat to see to it that the above measures are actually implemented.

This effort, like the IAEA's own review of the evidence regarding Iran, would likely take several months. During this period, though, there would be a presumption against any state taking any step to violate or undermine the NPT. Beyond this, it also would increase U.S. and allied leverage to get Iran to reconsider its nuclear program, and increase international support for isolating Iran if it continues to develop nuclear weapons-related capabilities.

2. Encourage Iranians to debate the merits of their nuclear power program and support of terrorism. As has already been noted, Iran could possibly have its first uranium bomb in as little as 2 years. It will take some months, at best, to get the IAEA and the UN Security Council to determine Iran's compliance status and to impose sanctions as appropriate. Whatever the outcome of these international efforts, though, the United States and its allies need separately to explain what Iranians can expect from a U.S.-led coalition if Iran continues its nuclear power program (which effectively assures Iran a nuclear weapons option) and retains its ties to terrorist organizations. At the same time, the United States and its key allies should also explain what benefits Iranians can expect—improved relations with the West that include a lifting of sanctions, major power security guarantees, energy aid, enhanced trade relations with Europe, and formal diplomatic relations with the United States—if they drop their ties to terrorists and end their nuclear power activities.

A key requirement for receiving any benefits would be for Iran to dismantle its nuclear power-related facilities in a verifiable way. The dismantling of these facilities would have to commence before these facilities could ever produce their first bomb's worth of uranium or plutonium, i.e., before the end of 2005. If Iran did this, the United States and its key Western allies should ease work visa regulations to help absorb the many Iranian nuclear technicians that would otherwise be without work. Iran would also have to cut ties to terrorist organizations. Here the potential nexus between terrorism and nuclear weapons figures largely. Certainly, if Iran comes within weeks of being able to have a large arsenal of nuclear weapons, it will only feel more confident in sheltering and supporting terrorists, the harboring of which would otherwise make Iran a potential military target. There also is the prospect that Iran might actually share its nuclear knowledge with these organizations. In this case, Iran could use these groups as strategic proxies to pose the very nuclear threats—against the United States, Iran's neighbors, and Israel—that Iran's own acquisition of a weapons option would otherwise accomplish. Also, as long as Iran keeps its ties to these terrorist organizations, it can always arm them with chemical or biological agents and other explosives, even if it abandons its nuclear power-related activities. With these arms, terrorists could accomplish many of the same goals that the United States and its allies fear these organizations might with nuclear weapons. Getting Iran to cut its terrorist ties, as such, is no less critical than getting it to end its nuclear weapons relevant activities.

Who should take the lead in explaining these points to Iran—Washington, the EU, Russia, or the P-5—and how these points would be presented, would have to be worked out.

As a compliment to this effort and to increase the credibility of the benefits Iranians could expect if they did drop their nuclear power program and terrorist support, the United States should launch a long-term outreach effort to the Iranian people (particularly those unhappy with the current style and substance of the current government's rule). The aim here would be to undermine the

Revolutionary government's demonization of the United States, which it uses to help justify its hostile, repressive policies. Achieving this objective will require persistent effort and should start with one or more of the following modest steps:

- Ease current travel restrictions on friendly Iranians visiting the United States. Under post-9/11 restrictions, Iranian dissidents and goodwill sports teams visiting the United States must be fingerprinted and photographed. In 2001, the Bush Administration allowed a wrestling team to enter the United States without fingerprinting. This was duly noted and appreciated. A way to make this outcome more likely and predictable is needed for desirable Iranian visitors. In addition, the United States should sponsor visits to the United States from Iranian journalists, prominent Iranian women, and Shia clergy.

- Provide logistical support for the direct broadcast of dissidents' messages into Iran. Given the recent Cuban jamming of broadcasts from Los Angeles, the U.S. Government should make available alternative secure means for these groups to reach their audiences. And it should provide material for use by private broadcasters and extend and expand the Voice of America television broadcasts in Persian, which have had difficulty securing stable funding.

- Make free instruction opportunities available over the internet. The Iranian government has had difficulty controlling the public's use of the internet to access Western sites and to communicate internationally. The United States and its friends should exploit this by offering the Iranian public a wide variety of internet educational courses tailored to their needs and desire for self-improvement. These internet courses should be offered free of cost from accredited recognized educational institutions and should lead to degrees to the extent possible.

- Expand disaster relief as required. This would not require a change in U.S. policy, only a more active effort to implement and properly publicize it.

- Provide counternarcotic assistance. The United States already is trying to stem the flow of Afghani drugs (the key source of Iranian drug users). It should augment these efforts and publicize what it has accomplished there. The UN Office for Drugs and Crime (UNODC) has an office in Tehran and is working to help reduce drug sales and use in Iran. Section 307 of the U.S. Foreign Assistance Act, however, prevents Iran from benefiting from U.S. contributions to international organizations. This prohibition has been waived for Iran in the cases of the IAEA and UNICEF. The President has not yet waived it for UNODC, though. This should be reviewed.

- Public health and health care assistance. Over 20,000 Iranians have contracted HIV/AIDs, mostly as a result of narcotics use. To address this growing problem, the United States could facilitate public health professionals' travel to Iran to assist in current World Health Organization (WHO) efforts to control this virus in Iran. More generally, the United States could expand its public health professional exchanges with Iran and work with local hospitals and doctors to establish the kind of computer-based public health monitoring systems currently being installed at very low costs in the United States and in NATO nations.

These efforts, which serve a number of political purposes (including reaching out to the possible future leaders of Iran) should be continued even if they fail to get the current government to reconsider its nuclear power program and support of terrorism. That said, if the rulers in Tehran fail to have a change of heart on these issues, the United States and its friends must be prepared for a much longer competition to turn Iran around. This longer competition would necessarily involve shoring up U.S. and allied security relations with Iran's neighbors (to limit the harm to regional and international security that Iranian nuclear threats might otherwise pose) and undermining Iran's confidence in the wisdom of its current policies.

3. If Iran continues to pursue worrisome nuclear activities, ramp up U.S. and allied military regional capabilities both to

neutralize the Iranian threat and forestall further proliferation. The United States and the military coalition in Iraq already must guarantee Iraq's security. Many of these same countries are also cooperating in efforts under the Proliferation Security Initiative to interdict nuclear weapons-related goods from reaching or leaving countries like Iran. Beyond this, the coalition needs to consult with the Gulf Cooperation Council states, Jordan, Turkey, Israel, and Egypt about their military plans for coping with a militant, nuclear (or near-nuclear) Iran. Certainly, Iran must understand that if it persists in developing its nuclear weapons option, it will face security costs and risks that would outweigh the possible value of acquiring nuclear weapons. At a minimum, plans should be made now on how additional military cooperation with Iran's neighbors (including intelligence sharing, missile defense cooperation, joint training, base sharing agreements, etc.) might best counter the threat and what new security arrangements, if any, would be appropriate. The general aim of these efforts should be to give Iran a choice between being outside of these arrangements (and a key reason for their establishment) or becoming an equal member by dropping its terrorist ties and becoming nonnuclear. Detailing what kind of security cooperation is desirable and clarifying the merits of overt and covert military action will be the focus of NPEC's follow-on analysis to be completed next spring.

CHAPTER 2

IRAN'S "LEGAL" PATHS TO THE BOMB

Victor Gilinsky

Introduction and Summary.

Recent events have reinforced the persistent suspicion that Iran seeks nuclear weapons. That suspicion is fed by Iran's drive to obtain all aspects of nuclear power technology, whether economically justified or not. Iran's strong emphasis on those technologies that would permit production of nuclear explosives—plutonium and highly enriched uranium—is especially worrisome. So is Iran's resistance to accepting more effective international inspections and, even more so, its likely violation of its current reporting obligations.

Iran's rationale for pursuing these technologies is that they would support the operation of its nuclear power reactors for generating electricity. So far, Iran has only one Russian-supplied unit, Bushehr 1, under construction. But it looks more and more as if the country—that is to say, the directorate of the nuclear program—has more in mind than generating electricity. Consider, for example, the issue of plutonium. The Bushehr reactor, like any uranium-fueled power reactor, would produce militarily-significant amounts of plutonium in its fuel during operation. Under U.S. pressure to make sure the plutonium from Bushehr did not end up in bombs, the Russians have agreed to take back the reactor's radioactive spent fuel, 1 percent of which would produce plutonium during the reactor's operation. Most power reactor operators are delighted to get rid of their spent fuel. The contained plutonium has no economic value. Iran, however, has made it clear that it intends to pursue reprocessing technology to separate the plutonium from spent fuel, which raises questions about the future of that Bushehr product.

As was revealed in August 2002 by an opposition group, Iran is also building a heavy water plant at Arak.[1] Iran has since informed the IAEA it intends to build a heavy water reactor, which would be even more suited to producing plutonium.

Iran is also opening the door to producing the other nuclear explosive of interest—highly enriched uranium.[2] Bushehr, like all water-cooled power reactors, would use low enriched uranium as fuel that Russia would normally supply. Yet in August 2002 it was brought to light by the same Iranian dissidents that Iran was building uranium centrifuge enrichment plants.[3] These cannot remotely be justified economically on the basis of Iran's nuclear power program. They would, however, be of major importance for producing nuclear weapons. The secretiveness about these plants during their early development is unsettling. Even more unsettling is the likelihood that Iran violated its safeguards agreement with the International Atomic Energy Agency (IAEA) in testing its pilot enrichment plant.

Likely IAEA Reporting Violations.

Iran, as a consequence of its adherence to the Nonproliferation Treaty, was obligated to inform the IAEA if it tested its centrifuges with uranium hexafluoride gas. It did not so inform the IAEA. It now asserts it used other gases for testing. It is, however, very difficult to believe Iran's assertion that it built its pilot centrifuge cascade and launched a huge centrifuge complex construction project without testing its unit design with the real stuff, so to speak. Such an omission would have violated all normal engineering practice. Moreover, Iran has resisted IAEA efforts to take environmental samples at the facility to check on Iran's claim.[4] Iran insists that it is not obligated to permit such sampling since it has not signed the Additional Protocol requested by the Agency of all its members.

There are a number of other IAEA reporting failures and activities that have raised concern:[5]

- In 1991, Iran imported 1.8 tons of natural uranium and failed to report it to the IAEA. Iran said it was not legally required to report it. The IAEA said Iran must declare all such imports "as soon as possible."

- Iran informed the IAEA in May that it intended to build a heavy-water research reactor at Arak, the existence of which the IAEA learned about in 2002 from media reports. This plant would yield weapons-grade plutonium.

- Iran has converted natural uranium into uranium metal. The IAEA says "the role of uranium metal . . . needs to be fully understood, since neither (Iran's) light water reactors nor its planned heavy water reactors require uranium metal."

Resisting the IAEA Additional Protocol.[6]

Adding to long-term suspicions is that Iran has been also unwilling to accept advanced IAEA safeguards—the so-called Additional Protocol that most countries have signed—that would permit more extensive inspection by the Agency.

The Additional Protocol (based on INFCIRC/540 [corr.]) is, according to the IAEA, the key to its strengthened safeguards system. Signers agree to provide the IAEA with broader information covering all aspects of its nuclear fuel cycle-related activities, including research and development and uranium mining. They must also grant the Agency broader access rights, including short notice inspections of all building at nuclear sites. They must also allow the IAEA to use advanced verification technologies, including environmental sampling.

The new Protocol would also allow the Agency to obtain more and earlier design information. The current requirement is that the IAEA is to obtain such information "as early as possible" without specifying a definite time.[7]

Iran recently said it would accept such a protocol if the United States and other countries would relax current restrictions on nuclear technology exports to Iran.[8] The United States would not agree for obvious and sensible reasons.

Is the Civilian Program Only a "Cover"?

There is still a tendency, even among those convinced Iran is intent on getting nuclear weapons, to see the country's nuclear power program as a *cover* for a separate clandestine weapons program rather than part of a weapon program and to fail to appreciate the nuclear explosive production capacity of the "civilian" program itself, especially that of the Russian-supplied Bushehr power reactor nearing completion.[9] Weapon design and preparation for weapon fabrication would, of course, have to be under cover, at least so long as Iran remains a member of the Non-Proliferation Treaty (NPT). Clandestine nuclear explosive production activities may take place, too. Still, it is not generally appreciated just how close Iran's planned nuclear program brings that country to a bomb. And not only would these activities—entirely legal under the current interpretation of the NPT so long as the IAEA can inspect them—bring Iran to the threshold of a bomb, but to the capacity for producing large numbers of them.[10] This report will provide estimates of the formidable potential of the reactor and related fuel cycle facilities.

Brief Background to Iran's Nuclear Program

Iran was one of the first signers of the NPT. From the first, however, Iran exemplified the hypocrisies embedded in the Treaty. The Treaty started as an effort among non-nuclear states to stem the spread of nuclear weapons capabilities. In its final form it became a deal between the haves and have-nots—the have-nots would promise to forego nuclear weapons and allow the IAEA to inspect their nuclear facilities (a promise reversible on 90 days' notice) in return for full access to all peaceful applications of nuclear technology just short of bombmaking. The Shah ratified the NPT in 1970 and soon after that started planning a grandiose nuclear power program that at one point included 23 nuclear power plants. It appears though that the Shah had more in mind than generating electricity and that he also started a secret nuclear weapons research program at about the same time.

All this came to a halt with the 1979 Islamic revolution and the Shah's departure. The new rulers apparently revived nuclear activities in the mid-1980s, when reports once again reached the West of bomb-related interests on the part of Iran. Unlike Iraq, which tried (and failed) to produce nuclear explosives by means of a secret

26

nuclear weapons project outside of the "declared" sector subject to IAEA inspections, Iran has skillfully exploited the weakness of the NPT. There is nothing illegal from the point of view of the Treaty, for example, in separating plutonium from irradiated reactor fuel, or in producing enriched uranium, so long as the facilities are accessible to IAEA inspectors. Since obtaining the nuclear explosive material is the most difficult part of making a bomb, this permissiveness allows a would-be bombmaker to get very close to his goal. And since an illicit bomb design and manufacturing capability is relatively easy to hide—it does not involve nuclear materials—it can be prepared secretly in parallel with overt explosive material production, so that when the material is ready it can almost immediately be put to bomb use.

That is the assumption the IAEA uses, at least in principle, for the purpose of guiding the timing of its own inspections. Article 28 of the current IAEA-Iran agreement states the "timely detection" principle:

> The objective of the safeguards procedures set forth in this part of the Agreement is the timely detection of diversion of significant quantities of nuclear material from peaceful nuclear activities to the manufacture of nuclear weapons or of other nuclear explosive devices or for purposes unknown, and deterrence of such diversion by the risk of early detection.[11]

The IAEA estimates that once in possession of the explosive material, a country that is so inclined and has made the necessary preparation in design and manufacturing capability can produce bombs *in a week or two*.[12] Interestingly, the IAEA then sets a goal for inspection frequency for holders of such materials at a month, and even that goal is not met consistently. Obviously, the Agency has given up the ability to provide "early warning" of an attempt to make one or a small number of bombs, and has relied on the deterrence effect of its ability to detect a larger bomb manufacturing effort within a month or so of the start of bomb manufacture. The effectiveness of a deterrent based on such a delayed unmasking of a would-be bombmaker is very much open to question.

Plutonium: Iran's Light Water Reactor at Bushehr.

The light water reactor that Russia is building for Iran, and of which Iran would like to get additional units, is a copious source of plutonium. This plutonium would not be difficult for Iran to extract. Too much has been made of the difficulty of reprocessing light water reactor (LWR) fuel, especially by a country with Iran's industrial base.[13]

The Bushehr nuclear power station based on the Russian LWR, with an electric generating capacity of 1,000 megawatts, is apparently nearing completion and the builders say it will be ready for fueling and testing within a year. Once it starts commercial operation it could produce—like any reactor of its type—about 250 kilograms of plutonium a year in the reactor's fuel. The significance of such an amount is obvious when one considers that the amount needed for a bomb is several kilograms.

To avoid accusations that they are helping the Iranians produce bombs, the Russians have said they have arranged to take back the reactor's spent fuel. In fact, they say they will *pay* Iran to get it back, which is a very unusual arrangement considered from a commercial

Figure 1. Bushehr Light Water Reacter.

point of view. Usually, operators of nuclear plants welcome any opportunity to ship it elsewhere. The fact that the Russians had to agree to pay for the spent fuel suggests the Iranians were not eager to get rid of it. The Iranians apparently forced the Russians to pay blackmail in order to revise their contract to one that would protect them against charges of contributing to weapons capabilities in Iran, which raises concerns all by itself. In any case, it is uncertain how such a spent fuel repatriation scheme would work and how effective it would be in the event the Iranians decided they wanted to stop shipping fuel to Russia. The arrangement has been thrown further into question by Iran's statement that it intends to acquire the capability to reprocess LWR fuel to extract plutonium, a capability it would not need to operate the nuclear units economically, and would have no use for if the spent fuel is to return to Russia.[14]

Despite the obvious plutonium production potential of the Bushehr reactor, the conventional concern about how Iran might obtain nuclear weapons has not centered on that plant. It has been that it might conduct a clandestine nuclear weapon program in the "shadow" of its civilian nuclear electric power program. For example, a Washington think-tank report on Iran, written in 2000, says the following under the heading of "Reactors and Proliferation":

> It not clear that Iran's reactor purchases are meant to be an integrated part of Iran's nuclear weapons effort, as distinguished from a way of acquiring the necessary nuclear technology. The reactor design Russia is selling Iran produces only very limited amounts of plutonium, and no country has as yet used a similar reactor design to acquire fissile material.[15]

Central Intelligence Agency (CIA) congressional testimony at about the same time conveys pretty much the same message:

> Work continues on the construction of a 1,000-megawatt nuclear power reactor at Bushehr that will be subject to International Atomic Energy Agency (IAEA) safeguards. This project will not directly support a weapons effort, but it affords Iran broad access to Russia's nuclear industry.[16]

Plutonium from Bushehr (in fact, from all LWRs) is more significant for weapons use than generally appreciated. A recent

Livermore report calculates that such a reactor can produce about 300 kilograms (about 50 bombs' worth) of near-weapon-grade plutonium produced by the first refueling—about 15 months after startup.[17] As mentioned earlier, the difficulty of extracting such plutonium from the radioactive spent fuel in which it is embedded has also been exaggerated. As put in an earlier 1995 Livermore report, the plutonium "can be separated from spent fuel with *modest facilities and equipment.*" [18]

The utility of bombs made from such near-weapons grade plutonium ("first cycle plutonium," from LWR spent fuel removed after one normal operation cycle) does not differ much from that of so-called weapons grade plutonium. The difference comes from the higher content of the plutonium-240 isotope (14 percent in the first-cycle plutonium as opposed to about 6-7 percent in weapons grade). The plutonium-240 fissions spontaneously, thus releasing neutrons to start a premature chain reaction in the fissile plutonium-239 as it is compressed in a detonating warhead. The random plutonium-240 spontaneous fissions introduce an uncertainty in yield because the premature chain reactions do not produce the maximum yield. The same problem affects the weapons grade material, only to a lesser extent, at least at the relatively basic weapons design level we assume here.[19] (The problem more or less goes away in advanced weapon designs.) Calculations on the performance of near-weapons grade plutonium performed for NPEC show that—using technology not much beyond that of the first U.S. weapons—the probability is high of attaining yields above the low kilotons with this material. The mean yield would be about 10 kilotons and the probability of exceeding a yield of about 20 kilotons would be about one-third, more or less the yield of the bombs dropped on Japan. [20]

The previously cited 1995 Livermore report stated more generally that "reactor-grade (RG) plutonium, such as that produced in commercial power reactors (after three fuel cycles rather than one as assumed above and thus of lower utility), can be used to construct a nuclear weapon with a yield of *at least a kiloton.*" The results cited here for the first-cycle plutonium describe performance considerably better than this.

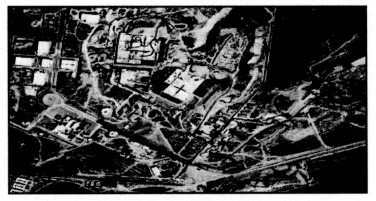

Figure 2. Enrichment Plant Construction.

Uranium Enrichment.

Iran is also developing uranium enrichment technology. It has pilot centrifuge facilities and has plans for building fairly large plants. Iran's claim is that it is interested in uranium enrichment for the production of LWR fuel. The centrifuges in the enrichment plants could also easily be reconfigured to produce highly enriched uranium.

It came as a surprise to the IAEA, and apparently to intelligence agencies as well, that Iran has a substantial uranium enrichment program. It took dissident groups within Iran to directed intelligence to a pilot plant at Natanz. The IAEA visited this plant and found a pilot facility using a cascade of more than 100 centrifuges. The IAEA officials reported seeing components for about another 1000 centrifuges. There are now public photographs available of a larger facility being built partially underground with two meter thick walls. It isn't clear whether the technology was an indigenous adaptation, or whether another country supplied it. An obvious candidate is Pakistan.

Weapons Significance of the Enrichment Facilities Iran is Building and Planning.[21]

To get an idea of the scale of Iran's uranium enrichment capacity and its significance in terms of weapons, it is useful to consider the enrichment capacity that is needed to support the refueling of a single large power reactor of the type the Russians are building at Bushehr. This requires a technical digression on the subject of enrichment as it applies here. Readers uninterested in the technical details can skim to the result without loss.

The core of a typical 1000 megawatt LWR such as the Bushehr reactor contains about 75 tons of low enriched uranium (LEU) fuel, a third of which is replaced at each refueling, about every 18 months. That means the requirement for fresh LEU fuel amounts to about 17 tons per year. Such LWR fuel is typically enriched to about 3-4.5 percent in uranium 235. (Recall that natural uranium contains about 0.7 percent uranium-235, the rest being uranium-238.) For the purpose of this calculation let us assume the fuel enrichment is 3.6 percent uranium-235.

Enrichment capacity is expressed in units of "separative work units" (SWU)–kilograms per year, or sometimes in tons SW per year. (These kilograms and tons are *not* amounts of material—unfortunately a somewhat confusing point.)

To produce 17 tons of 3.6 percent LEU fuel requires about 75 tons of separative work per year.[22] The separative work requirement is not precise because it depends on how the enrichment plant is run. This result assumes that the plant feed is natural uranium at 0.7 percent uranium-235 and that the "tails assay," the enrichment of the rejected material, is at 0.3 percent uranium-235. By raising the tails assay, by "skimming the cream" of a larger amount of feed material, one can reduce the amount of separative work required.

The total enrichment capacity of the plant is the sum of the individual enrichment capacities of the components—in this case, centrifuges. If we assume a nominal individual centrifuge capacity of 5 kilograms of separative work per year (or 5 SWU per year), such a plant would contain about 15,000 centrifuges. This is roughly in the range, within a factor of two or three, that the Iranians seem to be talking about for the large plants that are in the initial stages of construction.

Now consider how much highly enriched uranium such a plant could produce if the centrifuge cascade—the grouping of individual centrifuges—is reconfigured for that purpose. A similar enrichment calculation, assuming natural uranium feed and a 0.3 percent tails assay, shows that the same plant reconfigured could produce nearly 400 kg of 90 percent uranium-235, say 20 bombs' worth, per year.[23]

Using LEU as Feed Material Reduces Need for Enrichment Capacity.

Even more interesting is the possibility of using LEU as feed, that is, starting with uranium already enriched to, say, 3.6 percent rather than starting with natural uranium. Such low enrichment uranium could be either material imported for fueling LWRs or material previously enriched in Iran. Perhaps counter-intuitively, it turns out that most of the separative work to obtain HEU is already done in bringing natural uranium to the level of LEU because there is so much material to deal with at the lower enrichment levels. It turns out that if one starts with LEU feed, the nearly 400 kilograms of HEU per year (at about 90 percent uranium-235) could be turned out by an enrichment plant with a capacity of slightly over 15 tons SW/yr, or about *one-fifth* of the capacity needed for starting with natural uranium feed. This calculation assumes a 1.5 percent tails assay and therefore 16 tons of LEU feed per year, or about the amount of LEU needed annually to fuel a reactor of the Bushehr type. With a lower tails assay the separative work requirement would go up but the feed requirement would go down, and similarly for the reverse.

The separative work requirements scale with the amount of product. Starting with LEU, a smaller quantity of HEU, say, 100 kilograms of HEU per year, enough for about five nominal bombs per year, could be produced by a plant with an enrichment capacity of less than 4 tons of separative work per year. With the same assumptions as used previously that would amount to less than 1000 centrifuge units, roughly the level of equipment that the IAEA inspectors saw on hand in the form of components in a recent visit to Iran.

Summary: Iran's Two "Legal" Paths to Nuclear Explosives.

To summarize, the technical possibilities, all "legal" under the NPT, include both plutonium and highly enriched uranium. In terms of physical capability, once Bushehr is operational, which is slated for the end of 2004, Iran would have the possibility of using the Bushehr reactor plus a reprocessing capability it would have to develop. That could give it a bomb capability to produce dozens of warheads, though likely no earlier than, say, 2006. Another possibility, in light of Iran's construction of a heavy water plant, would base a military plutonium production capability on a heavy water reactor, but that could only come to fruition several years later.

The other, or possibly complementary, course would be based on highly enriched uranium produced in centrifuge plants, either the known plants or clandestine ones. A very small facility involving, say, 1,000 machines of modest capability, that could probably be hidden effectively, could produce several HEU warheads a year. If Iran made full use of a larger facility of the sort it appears to be building, the bomb production capacity would scale accordingly.

Of course, either course would involve treaty violations from which would follow diplomatic and possibly military consequences. The violation would not be mitigated by a withdrawal from the treaty. A country cannot legally gain the fruit of treaty adherence by accumulating the wherewithal for a bomb and then withdrawing. (That reflects a standard principle in contracts, but it would be helpful if the NPT members would say so explicitly.)

Changing the System of Protection in Terms of Allowable Technology, Inspections, and Enforcement.

Iran illustrates the vulnerabilities of the current international system of protection against proliferation. A major difficulty is that the present international norm is too permissive. The NPT has been read to say that all technologies and materials are acceptable so long as the owners declare them to be peaceful and allow IAEA inspection. But we know it is dangerous to allow members to get arbitrarily close to a bomb, or to have nuclear explosives around that others could steal. So we have tried to plug the holes in the treaty with various export controls over what we delicately call "sensitive" technology. Yet if North Korea had not been so foolish as to cheat, but instead had let the IAEA watch its pre-1992 reprocessing, there would not have been grounds for objection, at least under the treaty. Iran has taken a more sophisticated approach and is cleverly exploiting the weaknesses of the NPT. We cannot keep our fingers in the nuclear dike forever. We need a rule that limits what is acceptable in terms of civilian nuclear power technology to that there is a greater safety margin between it and possible military application. It will likely have to be a common rule applicable to all. That may sound unrealistic, but the alternative is unsustainable.

The once-through LWR fuel cycle is sometimes called "proliferation-resistant." It is a considerable improvement, in terms of security, over some of the alternatives, but it has its problems, too, and requires a very tight system of inspection, at least in suspicious places. At a minimum we need the upgrading in IAEA inspections that would follow from adoption of the "Additional Protocol" that most countries have signed and Iran has resisted.

Improved inspection will not be worth much as a deterrent unless behind it is a credible and effective reaction to violations. It used to be said years ago that, whatever the deficiencies of IAEA inspections, if there was ever a serious violation, there would be an immediate and tough international response. We have discovered enforcement is a complicated matter and there are always reasons to hold off. Consider the North Korean affair that has dragged for over 10 years after the IAEA found a serious violation. A chief problem is that the NPT has no enforcement mechanism so the matter is left to individual members. We need some kind of permanent international arrangement.

ENDNOTES - CHAPTER 2

1. State Department briefing, May 9, 2003. *http://www.state.gov/r/pa/prs/ps/2003/20439.htm*.

2. Highly enriched uranium (HEU) is uranium enriched in the isotope uranium 235 (the fissile fuel and explosive). For weapon use the proportion of uranium 235 has to be over, say, 80 percent. Natural uranium contains only about 0.7 percent uranium 235 and about 99.3 percent uranium 238. The uranium 238 is more or less inert in this context but when irradiated by neutrons, as it would be sitting in an operating power reactor, it can get turned into plutonium 239, the other nuclear explosive. Water-cooled power reactors use low enriched uranium (LEU) fuel with about 4 percent uranium 235. Most of the world's LEU is enriched in large plants in the United States, Russia, and Europe. The water-cooled reactors

are called LWRs, or light water reactors, to distinguish them from heavy water reactors.

3. U.S. intelligence apparently first learned of previously secret nuclear facilities—including a uranium enrichment plant at Natanz based on centrifuge technology—from an Iranian opposition group. If that is correct, it raises questions about the quality of U.S. intelligence.

4. *Reuters* dispatch from Tehran, June 12, 2003. "In a confidential report obtained by *Reuters* in Vienna last week, the IAEA said it had requested permission to take samples at a workshop at Kalaye where Iran had admitted to constructing components for centrifuges designed for enriching uranium."

5. *Reuters* report from Vienna, June 15, 2003.

6. IAEA Safeguards factsheet, *http://www.iaea.org/worldatom/Periodicals/Fact sheets/English/S1_Safeguards.pdf.*

7. The Text Of The Agreement Between Iran And The Agency For The Application Of Safeguards In Connection With The Treaty On The Non-Proliferation Of Nuclear Weapons, entered into force on May 15, 1974. Article 42, contains the following:

> Pursuant to Article 8, design information in respect of existing facilities shall be provided to the Agency during the discussion of the Subsidiary Arrangements. The time limits for the provision of design information in respect of the new facilities shall be specified in the Subsidiary Arrangements and such information shall be provided as early as possible before nuclear material is introduced into a new facility.

8. *United Press International*, Tehran, Iran, May 30, 2003. Iranian Foreign Minister Kamal Kharrazi said on Friday Iran would sign the Additional Protocol pertaining to the International Atomic Energy Agency if sanctions against it were lifted and nuclear technology for peaceful purposes was put at its disposal, the official Islamic Republic News Agency reported.

9. For background on the Iranian nuclear program, see Nuclear Threat Initiative web site at *www.nti.org*. The CIA addresses the issue of the possibility of an Iranian nuclear weapons program in a periodic report to Congress. A recent edition contained an increased appreciation of the significance of Iran's planned fuel cycle facilities: Unclassified Report to Congress on the Acquisition of Technology Relating to Weapons of Mass Destruction and Advanced Conventional Munitions, July 1 Through December 31, 2001, CIA, January 2003.

10. In this connection, a June 11, 2003, *Reuters* report from Tokyo states "Iranian experts on nuclear issues secretly visited North Korea this year, possibly to ask North Korean officials for advice on how to handle international inspectors, a Japanese newspaper said on Wednesday."

11. The Text Of The Agreement Between Iran And The Agency For The Application Of Safeguards In Connection With The Treaty On The Non-Proliferation Of Nuclear Weapons, Entered Into Force on May 15, 1974.

12. IAA Safeguards Glossary (2001), p. 22. See *www.iaea.org*.

13. The issue arose in the context of the U.S.-supplied LWRs for North Korea (built and mostly paid for by South Korea) that were part of the 1994 U.S.-DPRK Agreed Framework, and which in many ways parallel the Russian-supplied LWR for Iran. The State Department decried the Russia-Iran deal but defended the U.S.-DPRK one, ultimately on the claim that the DPRK wouldn't be able to extract the plutonium produced in the LWRs, a pollyannaish assumption.

14. Khatami speech February 9, 2003.

15. A. H. Cordesman, "Iran and Nuclear Weapon," Centerfor Strategic and International Studies (CSIS) report, 2000. This report, available at *http://www.csis.org/mideast/reports/irannuclear02072000.pdf*, contains a good deal of interesting background.

16. Statement by John A. Lauder, Director, DCI Nonproliferation Center to the Senate Committee on Foreign Relations on Russian Proliferation to Iran's Weapons of Mass Destruction and Missile Programs, October 5, 2000.

17. Livermore, 2000.

18. 1995 Livermore report: "Extraction and Utility of Reactor-Grade Plutonium for Weapons" (U) (see for example, *http://www.thoriumpower.com/files/tech percent20plutoniumblications/reactor_plutonium.pdf*).

19 The first plutonium weapons—Trinity and Nagasaki—got around this by using plutonium that had only about 1 percent plutonium-240, which means it was extracted from uranium fuel that had been lightly irradiated. Even then, there was some slight chance that the weapon would produce a low yield.

20. The design improvement amounts to, in effect, a doubling of 1945 bomb assembly speed. Sixty years later, that should be within the capabilities of first-time entrant into the bomb club.

21 See, for example, *http://www.urenco.de/trennarbeit/swucal_e.html*.

22. Not to be confused with the mass of the uranium core which happens to have the same figure.

23. The exact number is 388. The figure is rounded to 400 because the numbers are all approximate. The bomb equivalent assumes a nominal 20 kg of Uranium-235 per warhead.

CHAPTER 3

IRAN'S INTERNAL STRUGGLES

Geneive Abdo

Overview.

This chapter argues that prospects for fundamental reform, much less outright revolutionary change, in the Islamic Republic of Iran are minimal in the short- to medium-term. In the complete absence today of any coherent, organized opposition and that of any competing ideology that could effectively challenge the continued clerical dominance, Iran's national struggle will remain for the foreseeable future a matter to be hashed out within the ruling coalition of "political mullahs" and lay revolutionary activists and other Islamic intellectuals. It is the members of this elite, known in contemporary Persian as "insiders," who together comprise the two primary political factions, labeled by the Western terms "reformers" and "hard-liners." The fate of the Iranian nation has remained exclusively within this carefully controlled circle since the consolidation of the Islamic Revolution, and there are no signs that either wing is prepared to open the door to meaningful participation by "outsiders" beyond the pale of the revolutionary discourse. As a result, any clues to the future of Iran must be found among the behavior, interests and ideology of the "insiders."

To show why this is the case, I will present a complex, interrelated set of religious, social and political factors shaping the nation's destiny. These include: the essence and dynamics of the ruling clerical caste, which is deeply divided among "hard-liners," "reformers," and quietist "traditionalists"; the structure of the Islamic state and the extraordinary concentration of executive and supervisory powers in the hands of the appointed supreme clerical leader; the failure of "internal reform" led by President Mohammad Khatami; and the complete lack of any legitimate or credible opposition political movement or cohesive ideological challenge to the current Islamic political system.

I will analyze both the pillars of Iranian stability that keep the conservative establishment in power and the institutions and forces that may come one day to threaten the regime. Throughout, I will argue that neither revolution nor fundamental reform is likely anytime soon. The profound reason for this deadlock lies in the central theological, not political, debate dominating contemporary Iran: The dream among some to modernize Islam and the ambition of others to establish a "pure" Islamic state have clashed, destabilizing the country and undermining the democratic promise of the Islamic revolution.

The result is a nation frozen in place, one that will remain so until these deep-set contradictions underpinning the state and its relationship to society are resolved. Is Iran to be a Shi'ite Muslim state ruled by clerics with a monopoly on religious truth? Or is it to be a republic under the will of the people, while remaining consistent with religious and cultural traditions? While the focus of this paper is exclusively on Iran, it is worth noting that this broader struggle—a struggle not of Islam versus the West, but of Islam versus Islam—is actively at play in postwar Iraq and across the broader Muslim world.

After detailing the factors listed above and discussing their implications for regime stability, I will explore some of the potential turning points that could alter this roadmap and accelerate any emerging demands for fundamental change. I will also identify some key events and developments that could alert U.S. policymakers and other Iran-watchers to possible changes in the religious, social, and political landscape. These include the upcoming struggle over the succession to Supreme Leader Ayatollah Ali Khamenei, which could well mark the beginning of the end of the "Khomeini generation"; the selection and approval of the presidential candidates for the 2005 elections; continued attempts by reformists, so far futile, to modify the legislative process at the expense of the clerical establishment and in favor of popular will; and the ability of the political elite to forestall the demands of the educated and growing numbers of post-revolutionary Iranians. Of course, exogenous events also shape any nation's destiny, particularly those of the magnitude of the U.S.-led military campaign to topple Saddam Hussein and his Baathist regime in neighboring Iraq. Although events on the ground are moving quickly, I will briefly outline the immediate impact and likely future effects of the Iraq war and its aftermath on Iran's domestic political scene.

Finally, I will discuss the implications of the expected course of Iranian affairs—most charitably seen as "muddling through" and deferring the most difficult political, social, and religious questions as long as possible—on one of the pressing issues facing Washington decisionmakers: Iran's relationship to the United States. It is worth noting that whenever its own core values are involved, Iran remains for the most part highly immunized against outside interference in both its domestic affairs and its foreign policy.

Domestic Politics: Islam versus Islam.

Amid the chaos of the 1979 Islamic Revolution and its dizzying aftermath, it is easy to lose sight of the fact that Ayatollah Khomeini was a radical—not just politically, but in *religious* terms. In the face of almost universal opposition among the handful of recognized senior Shi'ite theologians in Iran and Iraq, he single-handedly revolutionized the role of the clergy and stood the entire notion of relations between traditionally quietist Shi'ism and the state, corrupt by religious definition and prone to error and sin, on its head. Begun in the 1940s and refined in 1970 during his exile to the Iraqi holy city of Najaf, Khomeini's vision extended the clergy's traditional authority over orphans, the insane or anyone else unable to fend for himself—an established principle known as *velayat*, or guardianship—to society as a whole.

Against the traditional role for the clerics as moral guides and intercessors on behalf of the people with an inherently corrupt political authority, Khomeini proposed that the clergy should assume direct political power, in what would become the first theocracy of the modern age. In other words, the clergy and the state would become one and the same. To the majority of Shi'ite thinkers this was blasphemy; the sacred texts make it clear that with the final disappearance of the last of the community's rightful leaders, the

41

sainted 12 Imams, in 941 AD, no mere mortal could unite temporal and religious authority in one office. Nonetheless, Khomeini pressed ahead, skillfully exploiting the weakness and divisions among both his clerical and secular opponents, with a speed and finality that surprised even his most ardent supporters; few if any had expected to live to see this blueprint for religious government enacted. With the ratification of Iran's new Islamic constitution in 1979, the principle of supreme clerical rule—the *velayat-e faqih*, or the guardianship of the jurisconsult—was established in law. It provides for an appointed senior Shi'ite cleric and expert in Islamic law to have final say over almost all state affairs, including control over the security forces and the right to declare war. These powers were further buttressed by constitutional revision in 1988-1989, in preparation for the succession after Khomeni's death.

The *velayat-e faqih* remains the most prominent feature of Iran's political system, providing the state with what its supporters say is an Islamic essence. Hard-line theoreticians refer to this system as a "guided" republic, to distinguish it from the liberal, democratic republics of the West, with the supreme leader and the many state organs he controls responsible for guiding the nation along the righteous path. This attempt to co-opt the established role of Shi'ite clerics as moral guides, however, has failed to win over traditional theologians, who abhor their fellow clerics wielding political authority. Practical-minded critics among them also point to the very real risk to the standing of the clerical caste once it assumes responsibility for the state; the inevitable failures and set-backs of statesmanship cannot but tarnish the clergy's standing in the eyes of the people. Finally, the traditionalists and many of their allies fear that Shi'ism is in danger of being reduced to a state ideology, a grave threat to a faith that has long prided itself on its independence, its intellectual rigor and its ability to adapt to the changing circumstances of life.

Together, these "traditionalists" make up by far the single biggest of the three clerical factions; the others are the "hard-liners" now in charge of the state, and the "reformists" seeking to liberalize and modernize—but not supplant—the existing Islamic order. True to their quietest credo, the traditionalists refrain from outward expression of their opposition to the *velayat*. What's more, these traditionalists—comprising a large body of senior clerics, their seminary students, and followers—could not be expected to ally themselves with any political reform that failed to respect Shi'ite religious and cultural values. Thus, they represent an unlikely source of anti-regime mobilization, although the steady accumulation of religious opposition to direct clerical rule may one day pose a serious threat to the legitimacy of the current order.

While the religious critique of supreme clerical rule dates back decades, more recently, the *velayat* has also become a target on political grounds among pro-reform clerics and many lay intellectuals, who see its present incarnation as a recipe for despotism and a violation of the democratic promise of the revolution. A number of former seminary students of Grand Ayatollah Hossein Ali Montazeri, a revolutionary-turned-dissident recently freed from house arrest for challenging the religious credentials of the present supreme leader, have developed a damaging critique of absolute clerical rule in an attempt to reform and modernize the Islamic political system. Most prominent among these are the mid-ranking clerics Abdollah Nouri and Mohsen Kadivar, the latter of whom was recently a visiting scholar at Harvard University.

Lay political activists, taking advantage of a brief period of press freedom during President Khatami's early years in office, brought the critiques of Kadivar, Nouri, and their allies from out behind the walls of the seminary and exposed them to the Iranian public for the first time. They also added their own opposition, drawn from their political commitment to expanded personal and social freedom, the rule of law and the need for a civil society within an Islamic order. Many are well-versed in the political philosophy of the West, which they have sought to harness for their own needs. At the same time, they are critical of what they see as the excessive freedom of the West and of its threat to traditional cultural and religious values.

These critics of the present clerical system advocate a greater degree of public participation in political life through a number of reforms that include: popular election of the supreme leader and the imposition of term limits on the office; watering down or removing the power to veto parliamentary legislation by the clerics of the Guardian Council controlled by the Leader; an end to the "vetting" of candidates for parliament and the presidency by this same council; the removal of direct clerical control over the judiciary; and the strengthening of the powers of the elected president, as a counter-weight to the appointed Supreme Leader. The result, say proponents, would be a fundamental rebalancing of the relationship between the people and the clergy and more representative of a true "Islamic republic," as envisioned by the broad coalition that overthrew the U.S.-backed Shah. Interestingly enough, many of these proposals were reflected in the first drafts of the post-revolutionary constitution (and some were drawn from the experience of the 1906-11 Constitutional Revolution), only to be lost in Khomeini's unexpected push for his maximalist demands of the *velayat-e faqih*.

After a period of disarray following the 1997 presidential landslide by the reformist cleric Mohammad Khatami, the hard-line establishment soon regained its footing. Relying on the organs of executive power under their control, chiefly the judiciary, the Guardian Council, and the security apparatus, they nullified the president's popular mandate for change and thwarted pro-reform legislation passed by parliament. Special clerical courts answering to the Leader, once dubbed the "Islamic Inquisition" by the pro-reform press, began the steady prosecution of religious dissent within the clerical ranks. Political opposition was quashed, with reformist leaders hauled before courts, thrown into prison or even murdered by death squads tied to the intelligence service. The leader and his circle also deployed gangs of religious zealots to break up political or religious protests, as well as the more formal Islamic militia, the *basij*. Both were used to great effect to ruthlessly suppress the July 1999 student protests that rocked Tehran and other major cities. By April 2000, the hard-liners felt sufficiently strong to undo the most noteworthy achievement of the Khatami era, forcing the mass closure of dozens of independent newspapers and prosecuting leading editors, publishers, and commentators. Not long after, the president publicly confessed he had no real power. The political critique of absolute clerical rule was forced back into the shadows, and the dream of reform among ordinary Iranians was in tatters.

Disillusioned with this failure, very few of Khatami's constituents bothered to vote in the latest municipal elections, which were held in March 2003, leaving the field to big conservative gains.

Nor is the regime likely to face any danger from the frequent but scattered economic and social protests that erupt regularly among ordinary people, often in the less developed towns, villages, and urban neighborhoods. These are generally provoked by a breakdown in municipal services, by corruption, or heavy-handed police tactics, fed by underlying frustration at persistently low living standards, high unemployment, and a widening disparity in income and opportunity. To date, such protests have been completely devoid of any political demands and there have been no attempts by the elites of any stripe to try to tap into this autarkic dissatisfaction.

In sharp contrast to the run-up to the Islamic Revolution, the fruit of a "theology of discontent" decades in the making among many classes and factions, domestic politics in Iran today remains very much restricted to the narrow circle of "insiders." I will discuss the failure of the reform movement in detail in Part IV below, but it is worth noting here that the unwillingness, or inability, of the so-called reformers to acknowledge or give voice to this popular discontent has doomed them to impotence. With the primary forms of potential opposition—theological, political and socio-economic— all muffled, Iran's national struggle has come down to an elite affair, best described as the struggle of Islam versus Islam.

The Structure of the State.

Iran's Islamic constitution provides an extraordinary concentration of executive power not in the hands of the elected president but in those of the Supreme Leader, or *vali-ye faqih*, appointed by a council of clerics dominated by hard-liners. In fact, the Iranian president wields less real power than perhaps any other elected chief executive in the world. This new constitution defines the Islamic Republic as a new kind of state, one ruled by qualified Islamic jurists until the missing Twelfth Imam, the last rightful ruler who disappeared in 941, makes his anticipated return to earth to usher in the age of perfect justice. The *vali-ye faqih* was given authority over the three branches of government, with specific

45

rights and duties detailed in Article 110. These include the right to appoint a Guardian Council, a body dominated by clerics to ensure parliament passes no laws or regulations in violation of the sharia, the Muslim holy law; supreme command over the military and the security forces, with the power to declare war and make peace; and the authority to confirm or reject the election of the president.

The Islamic constitution also creates a series of interlocking clerical bodies, ultimately controlled by the *vali-ye faqih*, at the expense of popular sovereignty as envisioned by many of Khomeni's lay revolutionary allies. In addition to the Guardian Council, which sits above the elected parliament and which has ultimate authority over both interpretation of the constitution and national elections, the law calls for a clerical Assembly of Leadership Experts, designed to select the leader and then supervise his work. Finally, the document mandates that all five seats on the Supreme Court and the office of prosecutor general be filled by Islamic jurists, with the head of the court and the prosecutor both direct appointees of the leader.

The completion of the final draft constitution by the Assembly of Experts, under the energetic leadership of Khomeini's star pupil, Ayatollah Mohammad Beheshti, bequeathed the world the first theocracy of the modern age. But the haste with which it was thrown together, with some delegates virtually tripping over one another to add more and more power to a supreme office earmarked for Khomeini, left the constitution a deeply flawed document, rife with legal shortcomings and outright contradictions. The most serious problems revolve around the remnants of a more liberal, democratic version, which can be found in the final document, only to be undermined elsewhere by the qualification that they be "consistent with Islamic standards." Specifically, these sections had to do with the rights and sovereignty of the people. Article 56, for example, notes that God alone exercises absolute power to rule over men, power that he has delegated to the people at large, not to the Islamic jurists. Other key articles also invoke the will of the Iranian people as the source of the state's legitimacy, as expressed in popular elections for president and the parliament. Finally, the text devotes considerable attention to the fundamental rights of the people, including freedom of expression, freedom of the press, and freedom to form political parties. None of these rights has ever been fully respected, but their very presence and the presence of other expressions of popular sovereignty have left Iran's political system unstable and subject to future challenges on both religious and political grounds.

With the end of his life drawing near, Khomeini came to realize that there were no prominent religious figures who could fulfill the political requirements of his office; after all, most of the senior clergy remained cool, to say the least, to the idea of religious government. So in a stunning about-face, Khomeini severed the connection between the most senior clergy—the sources of religious emulation—and the office of supreme ruler, a link that had always been presented as central to his conception of Islamic government. Khomeini ordered a revision of the constitution, creating by decree a special assembly to do the job. The mission was clear: rework the law of the land to pave the way for his designated successor, the mid-ranking cleric, Ali Khamenei. Article 109, requiring the leader to be selected from among the senior-most clerics, the *marjas*, was scrapped. Other articles that would have allowed for a collective clerical leadership, a return to idea of the clergy as a whole as the "general representative" of the Imams, were also jettisoned. The powers of the leader were strengthened further at the expense of the elected president, while the office of prime minister was eliminated altogether. The revisions also abolished the judicial council that oversaw the work of the courts and the prosecutors, replacing it with a single judiciary chief answering only to the leader. Further changes gave the *vali-ye faqih* explicit authority to delineate the general policies of the Islamic Republic and to supervise implementation of those policies, as well as the right to appoint the head of the state broadcasting monopoly.

This further centralization of power has left the institution of the *velayat-e faqih* virtually impregnable to any foreseeable political challenge. The pro-democracy student riots of July 1999, the worst social unrest since the aftermath of the revolution, provide an excellent case in point. Despite the fury of the street protests, which caught many at home and abroad by surprise, the regime had no real difficulty in suppressing the outbreaks and in ensuring that nothing on such a scale would be repeated anytime soon.

47

Nor did the students' demands for greater freedom of expression and less clerical interference in their daily lives resonate among the population at large or among the pro-reform "insiders," who immediately distanced themselves from the protesters. Relying on its total domination of the police and the security apparatus, as well as the volunteer Islamic *basij* militia and the less formal vigilante forces based in neighborhood mosques, the regime crushed the student protests in a matter of days. Brutal tactics, including beatings, torture, lengthy imprisonment, and the threat of death sentences, halted any incipient opposition movement in its tracks. Many Western observers took the student protests, however truncated, as a sign of a growing demand on the part of Iran's huge youth cohort for a secular society. In fact, my extensive interviews with campus activists and ordinary students during and after the July unrest made it clear the vast majority of educated youth were demanding greater social and political freedom *within* an Islamic context; they want an Islamic system, just not *this* Islamic system.

Khomeini's reworking of the constitution also reflects the often-overlooked flexibility of the ruling circles, another factor in their longevity. To justify the radical changes needed for a smooth handover of power after his death, the ailing leader cited the overriding need to ensure the survival of the Islamic political system. In doing so, he invoked the religious principle of expediency, or *maslahat*. Clearly, it was in the best interests of the Islamic Republic to have an orderly transition, even at the risk of undermining religious practice. Likewise, *maslahat* was at work when, in a direct slight to the established clerical system, Khamenei was given the title of ayatollah despite his lack of religious and scholarly credentials. To the chagrin of the clerical critics of the Islamic Republic, Khomeini and his allies had long resorted to *maslahat* whenever the practical needs or interests of the Iranian state clashed with the traditional teachings of Shi'ite Islam. This was as true for such fundamental issues as taxation and banking, on which religious law places explicit if inconvenient restrictions, as it was for the prohibitions against music and chess, both of which were later waived in the face of social reality. In one notable ruling, it was decreed that soccer players and wrestlers, who enjoy enormous popular followings in

Iran, were not in violation of religious law when they wore shorts or other immodest clothing required for their sport. Nor was watching such events on television or in person a violation of the *sharia*.

As tensions began to mount between the traditional reading of Islamic law, as championed by the Guardian Council, and the demands of modern legislation approved by the elected parliament, Khomeini was forced increasingly to step in to bridge the gap. In January 1988, he implemented a startling and far-reaching measure to protect his young republic, declaring that a genuine Islamic state had the right to disregard religious law when passing legislation. Whatever was in the interest—or *maslahat*—of maintaining the ruling Islamic order, he argued, represented the "most important of God's ordinances" and took precedence over all others "derived or directly commanded by Allah." One month later, he institutionalized this principle by creating an Expediency Council to determine the interests of state and break deadlocks between parliament and the Guardians. The Expediency Council, whose members are chosen directly by the leader, was also accorded legislative powers of its own. This new body, with the reliable Akbar Hashemi Rafsanjani at its head, was then given legal sanction in the revised constitution.

The enormous concentration of power in the hands of the establishment clerics, led by Khamenei and his allies, has provided the regime with more than enough tools to head off any challenge to its authority. It has also successfully thwarted the reform movement and its attempts to introduce greater popular participation and greater pluralism. After the unexpected setback of the 1997 Khatami landslide, the hard-liners soon realized they retained all the legal authority they needed to regain the upper hand, and they did so decisively. Their efforts were assisted by the mainstream reform movement, which, true to its "insider" roots and tone deaf to popular demands, declared at the outset its opposition to any attempt to revise the constitution. As a result, any significant reform will remain more a matter of negotiation within the narrow circle of competing elites than an endeavor fuelled by public demand, popular vote or protest.

The Failure of Internal Reform.

With deep structural change in the form of constitutional revision off the table from the start, the pro-reform movement with Khatami at its symbolic head nonetheless squandered perhaps the best chance in a generation for internal reform. With almost 70% of the popular vote in May 1997 for his reformist platform, Khatami failed to take advantage of the opening and the disarray among his hard-line rivals. Instead of pressing quickly to implement campaign pledges to introduce the rule of law and to begin building a civil society before the conservatives could regroup, the new administration and its allies settled for half-measures. A letter from a prominent member of the radical wing of the Khatami coalition argued the president-elect faced serious obstacles that could be addressed only by swift and resolute action. These recommendations included a major foreign policy address denouncing terrorism and proclaiming Iran's readiness for relations with all nations on the basis of mutual respect; creating true political parties; promoting freedom in the universities; introducing independent newspapers and radio and television stations; and banning the Islamic vigilante groups that oppressed society at every turn. With the exception of a policy of press freedom, all of the other measures were stalled or ignored completely; even the opening of independent newspapers—arguably the one short-lived success of the Khatami era—was seriously delayed by bickering within the reformist camp.

The March local elections in Iran marked the formal low point for the reform movement led by Khatami and his allies. During my almost 3 years in Iran, from 1998 to early 2001, the capital, Tehran, was a hotbed of pro-reform political activism. But this time, just 12 percent of eligible voters bothered to cast ballots, a far cry from the heavy turnout that characterized the president's first election, or later polls for local councils and parliament. Across Iran, candidates associated with Khatami fared poorly, while those aligned with the conservative faction gained strength, even capturing the high-profile office of Tehran mayor.

Such dismal results on the part of the reformist project should have come as no surprise. Their seeds, in fact, were sown as far back as the summer of 1999, when Khatami virtually turned his back on his most ardent supporters, the nation's university students who had taken to the streets to press the president's own demands for freedom and tolerance, and cast his lot with the ruling establishment. In a fateful address in the city of Hamadan on July 27, 1999, Khatami marked both the defining moment in his tenure and a turning point for the mainstream reform movement. A huge crowd of mostly male students crammed the local soccer stadium to await the president. Many chanted, "Khatami, we love you," under the baking sun; they were certain the president would endorse their aspirations and commiserate in their losses at the hands of the police and the vigilantes. But when he took the podium, Khatami stunned his audience with a strong endorsement of the *status quo*. Instead of instilling confidence in his foot soldiers, who had just risked their lives fighting in the streets for change, the president chose to rewrite the history of the pro-democracy protests, denying what many—including this author—had seen with their own eyes. "My dear ones, today in order to put down the riots and to put out the flames of violence for the nation, others use tanks, armored cars and heavy weapons. Our forces did not use firearms to tackle the rioting. The disturbance was put down calmly."

Khatami went on to dismiss the pro-democracy protests in Tehran as the work of thugs. "It was an ugly and offensive incident, which marred the image of our dear, patient, rational people . . . It was to express vengeance toward the system. It had nothing to do with the honorable nation or the university students." Many of the president's more militant supporters were stunned. Had not the students risked all to take their grievances beyond the walls of the universities and go directly to the people? Had they not protested to secure the very rights the president had affirmed was their legal due within the Islamic political system?

Over time, I watched as Khatami steadily abandoned his core supporters who had first put him in office—the religious intellectuals, including many prominent newspaper editors, publishers and commentators, as well as reform-minded clerics, feminists, and lay political activists. In one particularly poignant moment, two leading newspapermen, Mashallah Shamsolvaezin and Hamid Reza Jalaiepour sent a plaintive letter to the president, whose agenda they

51

had pushed relentlessly, asking for his protection from the hard-liners in the police and the courts.

These were brave men, ready to risk prosecution for their pro-reform convictions. Jalaiepour, a big, gregarious man, kept a kit bag with a razor and toothbrush by his desk in case he was hauled off by the police. And both did time in jail. Yet, they could not disguise their hurt and anger that they had been abandoned by the symbolic head of the reform movement. "Either tell us that our press activities are illegal . . . or tell us clearly from which government body we are to get a minimum of political and professional security to continue our work." They had taken Khatami at his word and pursued his promise of reform to its logical conclusions. With the police virtually knocking on their door, they asked, where was the president now? Khatami never responded.

When Election Day rolled around this March, millions of ordinary Iranians, who often took their cues from the political and cultural elite, voted with their feet and stayed away from the polls. How had it all gone so wrong?

At least four factors contributed to this failure. First, Khatami was a loyal product of the system he sought to reform. Second, his commitment to—and understanding of—the broader reform project and its theological, social, and political implications was always in doubt. Third, the obstacles to profound structural change, in particular those posed by the country's constitution that all but guaranteed the hold of the hard-line clerics, were enormous. And finally, the president and his allies failed to build a firm foundation for their proposed Islamic civil society, eschewing the time-consuming work of creating genuine political parties and grassroots organizations and instead relying on a sort of media campaign—in this case, the formation of an independent press—to carry the day.

On a cold winter day in 1997, Mohammad Khatami presented himself to Iran's supreme clerical leader at the latter's residence in Jamaran, once a village but now part of the sprawling capital, Tehran. He was considering a run for the presidency but had told his backers he was determined to give the leader, who has the final word in all matters of state, the chance to veto his candidacy from the start. He told Ayatollah Khamenei that his message of tolerance, pluralism, and openness could draw Iranians, who had grown increasingly apathetic and cynical, back into the political system. He would also reach out to women and ethnic minorities, broadening popular support for the Islamic system and, by extension, for the leader himself. The leader, like everyone else in Iran, assumed Khatami could never win, and he gave the candidate his blessing to run while making no comment on his election platform. The result was the landslide victory of May 1997.

It is important to recognize that the reforms that came to be associated with the campaign of 1997 and the person of Mohammad Khatami represent only one of several key strands that made up the coalition of clerics, workers, leftist militias, secular and religious intellectuals, Iranian nationalists and university students who carried out the Islamic Revolution almost 2 decades earlier. For years, any push toward greater democracy, pluralism, and the rule of law were subordinated first to the demands of consolidating the revolution and purifying society of Western influence, as well as to the struggle with the Great Satan in the aftermath of the U.S. Embassy takeover. The bloody Iran-Iraq war, which dragged on for 8 years, further retarded the nascent reform movement. It was only with the end of the war in 1988 and the death in 1989 of Khomeini—a man, his son records, who was broken by the failure to bring down Saddam Hussein—that the reformers began to find their voice.

However, the tensions within the Khatami coalition began to show within days of its stunning electoral victory. Activists like Shamasolvaezin and Jalaiepour were impatient to push the reformist agenda. They argued for the immediate creation of a political party and the formation of grassroots organizations. But they were vetoed by powerful rivals inside the Khatami camp, who feared alarming the clerical establishment and diluting their own political power. Instead, the two men, joined by the U.S.-educated engineer Mohsen Sazegara, poured their enormous energies into creating the first truly modern newspapers of the post-revolutionary era.

This was, it turned out, a fateful decision, for it represented the path of least resistance and distracted the reform movement from the more basic building blocks of their proposed civil society, such as true political parties and nongovernment organizations (NGOs).

For Khatami, himself a former newspaper publisher, and the other intellectuals and activists who supported him, the written word was a seductive device. A free press, they argued, would mobilize public opinion, act as a check on arbitrary state power, and energize a society beaten down by revolution, war, death, and suffering. Sports, Western movie stars, pro-reform clerics, and biting political commentary all competed for readers' attention. "We were thinking about happiness and life, instead of sadness and death—to publicize life," Sazegara told us. "We were thinking of a kind of renaissance by happiness." The result, the color daily newspaper *Jameah*, was a spectacular success. Daily circulation quickly hit 100,000, the paper's break-even point, on its way to 300,000 and beyond. Plans for an independent publishing house, a political club, and a lecture series, all affiliated with *Jameah*, began to take shape.

The hard-line authorities soon recognized the danger. The election of Khatami was bad enough, they reasoned, but the unbridled voice of a truly independent press was another matter all together. Backed by the supreme leader, the Tehran prosecutor closed the newspaper and its successor and jailed its founders. So began a game of cat and mouse between the pro-reform press and the hard-liners in control of the courts. Religious imperative was also invoked to silence dissent, and many editors and publishers were jailed on charges of violating Islamic values.

The early Khatami years saw an explosion of independent newspapers and journals. These publications introduced educated Iranians to the reformist ideas and modernist theological debate that had once been restricted to private reading circles or hidden behind the walls of the religious seminaries. Corruption at the highest levels was exposed, and the powerful chief of the feared secret service was brought down in a murder scandal uncovered by the press. But one by one, these newspapers and magazines fell to the entrenched power of the clerical establishment, which exercised power through the un-elected institutions under its control, chiefly through the judiciary. In April 2000, these "press wars" closed dozens of publications. Prominent editors, publishers and commentators were hauled before the courts. The crowning achievement of the Khatami years was over.

Seven months later, I sat in the audience as the president confessed before a conference of lawyers and religious jurists that he had failed. His campaign promises to introduce the rule of law and create a civil society had proven empty. "After three and a half years," a grim-faced Khatami said, "I must be clear that the president does not have enough rights to carry out the heavy task on my shoulders."

Markers and Roadmaps.

A number of factors and events bear watching by U.S. policymakers as they study the roadmap ahead. These include:

- The selection of presidential candidates for the election of Spring 2005. The Guardian Council of conservative clerics has established its right to vet all candidates for parliament and the presidency, and it has acted aggressively to defend the interests of the establishment. In 1997, it barred all but four of 238 hopefuls. A Council member told me the inclusion of Mohammad Khatami—whom virtually everyone, including the candidate and his inner circle, assumed would lose—among the finalists was the single biggest mistake in the panel's history. How will the hard-line clerics handle pro-reform candidates this time? Will they risk further alienating an already apathetic and dispirited electorate? Can they prevent a qualified lay candidate, or will they retain the clerical monopoly on the post?

- The eventual secession to the Supreme Leader. Born in 1939, Khamenei remains relatively young. He appears to have recovered from unknown health problems—rumors in Tehran included cancer but these could not be confirmed—that plagued him in the late 1990s and looks more vigorous than he was at that time. However, a smooth transition is vital to political stability. The steady loss of religious authority by the Leader's office suggests any successor would come from among the "political mullahs." Any deviation from this toward a figure more acceptable in religious terms, or a return to the earlier notion of a ruling clerical council in place of a single Leader, would be highly significant.

- The reform movement has mounted a series of so far unsuccessful challenges to the supervisory and veto powers of the hard-line clerics on the Guardian Council. A frustrated Khatami has repeatedly threatened to put the matter to public referendum, or even to resign, to break the deadlock between popular and clerical power. It is unclear whether such a referendum could be held at all, or what its impact might be. The resignation ploy appears a doomed gambit; the president has already lost so much credibility with ordinary Iranians, and he has issued similar threats before without following through. Any steps, however unlikely, to rebalance the relationship between the Islamic *state* and the Islamic *republic* are worth noting.

- More than half of the Iranian population is under 25, with no memory of the Islamic Revolution and little real recall, if any, of Khomeini. This second generation of the Revolution has little or no commitment to the values and ideals of the ruling elites. Many are well educated, thanks to an extensive university system, and the system must find a way to meet their economic, social, and political aspirations. However, it is vital to stress again that the common Western argument, that this generation has rejected Islam and yearns for a secular Iran, is completely without foundation. Rather, today's youth want greater freedom of expression, cultural and political pluralism, and more economic opportunity—attributes they believe are compatible with their religious and cultural values. How effectively will the regime absorb this new generation, or will it continue to sit back as the best and the brightest pursue opportunity overseas in a debilitating "brain drain"? Will this new generation make common cause with other disaffected elements of society? Or will its most ambitious members simply seek their place among the "insiders," a trend already visible among a number of campus leaders today?

Domestic Politics and U.S.-Iran Relations.

Despite more than 2 decades of hostility and the lack of diplomatic ties, the U.S.-Iranian relationship is a defining force in the foreign policy of the Islamic Republic. It also represents a huge, if often unstated, presence in the domestic affairs of the nation. Here in Washington, that primacy has long fostered the mistaken notion that the United States can exert considerable influence over the terms of any bilateral relationship and over Iran's internal affairs as part of any future rapprochement. In fact, the Islamic Republic is almost impervious to conventional outside pressure, particularly from the "Great Satan." Armed with its revolutionary and anti-colonial ideology and insulated against the general desire among ordinary Iranians for a resumption of ties, the ruling elite must sort out this matter within its own ranks.

Each faction is continually weighing the costs and benefits for itself—not for the nation—and calculating the risks and uncertainties involved. For example, the influential *bazaari* merchants, who dominate much of the domestic economy and enjoy close ties to the clerical establishment, are clearly tempted by the potential rewards of expanded foreign trade; but they also realize their dominant positions in commerce and capital formation could easily be overshadowed by a complete opening to the outside and the arrival of American banking giants. While most reformist politicians generally favor an end to Iran's isolation and xenophobic foreign policies, they remain deeply anti-American (many were former hostage-takers, and they have replaced the anti-British views of their forefathers with intense distrust of the United States). The Supreme Leader, often among the most shrill of anti-American voices, remains fearful that restored ties would undermine Iran's religious and cultural values. At the same time, each faction wants to be sure that it controls the relationship, in order to channel the benefits toward its supporters and to accrue the political gains for ending the deadlock. Only when a broad consensus is reached among these "insiders," will there be movement on the American front, and it will certainly not come at a cost of major concessions on the part of Iran.

This phenomenon underscores the futility of periodic U.S. overtures, often to the more pragmatic conservatives like former president Rafanjani ("a man we can do business with"), or to his successor Khatami, whose reformist platform has led many in Washington to see him as a "democrat" and thus a natural ally. It also invalidates the conventional wisdom among Western diplomats in Tehran that appeals to Iran's national interests will inevitably draw the country closer to the United States. A botched attempt by the Clinton White House to establish a secret channel to Khatami soon leaked to the conservatives, prompting the Supreme Leader to issue a blistering public attack on America and to launch a damaging witch hunt against Western "bases" among the reformist faction.

In February 2000, a U.S. message of congratulations to the reform movement for its relatively strong showing in parliamentary elections completely overshadowed the event itself. As a result, the reformers were forced to use their victory press conference, called to lay out an ambitious legislative agenda before the people and a huge international press corps, to assert their anti-American credentials and deny they were Western lackeys. Similarly, any goodwill from Secretary of State Madeleine Albright's attempt in March of that year to voice regret for the U.S. role in the 1953 coup that restored the Shah was completely squandered by references in that same speech to undemocratic elements among Iran's ruling circles, remarks that outraged the entire Iranian elite. The most recent attempt by Washington to shape the Iranian political landscape came last summer, with a declaration by President Bush that America was effectively abandoning any support for Khatami and the reform movement and calling on the Iranian people to overthrow their government. For the reasons outlined earlier in this chapteer, this bid will likewise fail.

If the troubled bilateral relationship and the Islamic Republic's domestic policies remain largely immune to overt U.S. suasion, then what of Iran's foreign policy? U.S interests and concerns lie in several specific areas: the possible export of the Islamic Revolution, with its model of authoritarian clerical rule; and Tehran's response to events in postwar Iraq.

The overthrow of the Shah and the rise of clerical power that followed deeply alarmed Muslim rulers across the Middle East, as well as their Western backers. Gulf states such as Saudi Arabia, Iraq, and Bahrain—all with sizeable and restive Shi'ite populations—were terrified that Khomeini's call for worldwide Islamic revolution threatened their grip on power. The authoritarian leaders of Sunni states like Egypt and Jordan, long denounced by Islamist activists as corrupt and religiously illegitimate, were also badly shaken. After all, the leader of the Islamic Revolution saw himself as the leading voice for the global *ummah*, or Muslim community of believers, rather than just a the new head of state. Millions of Muslims, both Shi'ite and Sunni, were inspired by the Iranian experience. Over time, however, this vision began to crumble under the weight of the Iranian model's declining religious authority, its practical setbacks in running a state, and the need to focus increasingly on domestic problems and issues. In the early 1990s, Supreme Leader Khamenei formally renounced the export of the revolution, and today Iran's relations with its neighbors are defined less by ideology than by traditional geopolitics.

While events in predominantly Shi'ite southern Iraq have reignited fears in some quarters of a resurgence of revolutionary fervor on the part of Iran, recent history suggests the Islamic Republic would be more than content to see a stable, non-hostile Iraq on its border, regardless of the structure or form of government there. And, in fact, Khatami said as much on his just-completed visit to Lebanon, where he held talks with state officials as well as with the leaders of the Shi'ite movement Hezbollah. The president called for a democratic Iraq, based on the principle of "one man, one vote." This mirrors the latest public comments by Ayatollah Mohammad Bakr al-Hakim, a Shi'ite cleric and the leader of the Supreme Council of the Islamic Revolution in Iraq (SCIRI).

Hakim fled to Iran after the failed Shi'ite rebellion, encouraged by Washington in 1991, against Saddam Hussein, and he directs a formidable political and militia organization. His status as an exile opposition figure in Tehran for more than a decade, before his return to postwar Iraq, often obscures the fact that Hakim and SCIRI are not simply puppets of their former hosts in Tehran. As the scion of a leading clerical family in the Iraqi holy city of Najaf, Hakim commands both religious and popular support, while SCIRI'S role in armed resistance to the Baathist regime has conferred considerable political legitimacy on the group. Hakim should not be viewed as a mere stalking horse for Iranian-style clerical rule in Iraq. Nor is he likely to seek any veto over a pluralistic postwar government.

On a more fundamental level, the fall of Saddam Hussein, who brutally suppressed the Shi'ite leadership, could open the way to a return of Najaf as a leading Shi'ite religious and intellectual center. The Iraqi city, site of the shrine to the Shi'ite saint, Imam Ali, had lost its standing in 1922 when its most active members were effectively forced out by the British. Many, including the young Ruhollah Khomeini, relocated to the sleepy Iranian town of Qom, which soon became a vital center of religious learning and later an important hub of revolutionary activity.

If Najaf once again regains its seat at the center of the Shiite world, a Qom-Najaf corridor would influence the role of Shiite Islam in the region and solidify the Shi'ite influence over a postwar Iraqi government.

Conclusion.

In conclusion, religion will continue to play an important role in the domestic affairs inside Iran and the region. The strength of the clerical establishment should not be underestimated. Thus, any notions that Iran is on the verge of a second revolution which would prompt the fall of the clerics is unrealistic. Such a proposition is put forth by Iranian ex-patriots whose secular orientation has blinded them to the realities of Iran over the last 2 decades. Similarly, the proposition that Iran's younger generation is awaiting the chance to overthrow the regime and could do so with a little push from the United States, is also a false assumption. For all the reasons stated in this chapter, Iran's youth are not seeking a secular state but rather a reformed Islamic system which takes into account their religious and cultural values while also meeting their needs in the modern world. Furthermore, history in Iran and the history of revolutions have shown that it takes far more than unhappy people to foment revolutions. A broad-based social movement, comprised of workers, secularists, students, and modernist clerics, would be necessary to carry out a revolution. Such a coalition is absent in Iran and there is no indication that one is on the horizon.

CHAPTER 4

THE PROSPECTS FOR REGIME CHANGE IN IRAN

S. Rob Sobhani

The people are very dissatisfied, and they are right to be so, and I swear to God that the society is on the brink of explosion. If this discontent increases, as is the case, the regime will be threatened.

> Ayatollah Ebrahim Amini
> Assembly of Experts
> (Power to Appoint
> Supreme Leader) 2002

Introduction.

The question before us today is: What are the prospects of Iran's revolutionary government giving way to reform or overthrow over the next 10-20 years? Furthermore, and more importantly for the United States, what groups and forces within Iran are opposed to the current revolutionary government and/or its efforts to develop nuclear power and long-range strategic weapons systems?

The purpose of this chapter is to demonstrate that **Iran's revolutionary government can be overthrown within 2 years** should the United States adopt a more robust policy of empowering the Iranian people to change the regime in Tehran. A regime change in Iran would put an immediate end to Iran's pursuit of weapons of mass destruction and instead focus the efforts of the new secular government on the domestic priority of pulling Iran out of its current Third World status. Equally important, the demise of the Islamic Republic of Iran at the hands of the Iranian people would send a very powerful message to the rest of the Muslim world that Islam, as a form of governance, has failed. The failure of political Islam would be a victory for the United States and our war against Islamic fundamentalism.

The end result of a more robust policy on Iran would allow

ent Bush to look the American people in the eyes and state the
ing: "On September 11, 2001, an arc of tyranny and dictatorship
ed from Afghanistan through Iran into Iraq. Today, an arc of
...n rules in Kabul, Tehran, and Baghdad. And the world is a
safer and better place as are the peoples of Afghanistan, Iran, and
Iraq."

Iran: Challenge and Opportunity.

Militant Islam is today's engine of international terror. Islamist
schools breed a new militant generation, Islamist sermons mobilize
opinion against the free world, Islamist ideology legitimizes recourse
to terror and Islamist "charities" bankroll the global network of
terror. While most Muslim states are aware of this threat to the
world and their own stability, there is one that is actually governed
by Islamists: The Islamic Republic of Iran.

Therefore, the principal component of the war against terrorism
should be the war against *militant* Islam, which over the last 20
decades has been inspired, nurtured, and funded by the Islamic
Government of Iran. The demise of the clerical regime in Iran would
go a long way in "draining the swamp" of militancy and radicalism in
the broader Muslim world with enormous geopolitical consequences
for U.S. national security interests. Therefore, the permanent success
of this campaign rests on a regime change in Iran.

In short, the United States faces two immediate timelines: one, the
mullahs' access to a nuclear bomb, and the other, institutionalization
of democracy through a regime change. The fundamental goal of
U.S. foreign policy should be the acceleration of the regime change
timeline.

In many respects, the people of Iran face a similar set of timelines.
The choices facing Iran over the next 10-20 years are simple: a
country relegated to permanent Third World status with a nuclear
bomb or an advanced, modern, secular country at peace with itself
and its neighbors.

The geopolitical interests of the United States coincide with the
interests of a majority of Iranians: a fundamental change in the nature
of the regime in Tehran. The overthrow of the Islamic Republic of
Iran is good for America and good for the Iranian people. Therefore,

Washington's strategy should be to support those forces inside and outside Iran which share America's political, economic, military, and geopolitical vision for the region. Towards this end, the United States must continue to isolate the clerical regime and encourage the growing spirit of rebellion among the repressed Iranians.

Assumptions.

1. Unwilling to pursue serious dialogue on normalizing relations with Washington, Tehran's foreign policy goal instead is to defeat the U.S.-led sanctions policy and to only engage the U.S. private sector (American energy companies, in particular). For this purpose, the apologists for the clerical regime have established well-funded "nonprofit" entities within the United States to soften Washington's tough stance against the clerical establishment.

2. Led by the 50 million youth, the demand for reform in Iran created President Khatami in 1997. In fact, the reform movement was created by the mass demand for change. However, his inability to deliver has broadened the mass discontent and accelerated the implosion of the clerical regime. The historic election of 1997 was a clear signal to the clerical establishment that Iranians want the freedom to live and prosper without "divine intervention," and that they want an end to their country's international isolation.

3. Despite official denunciations, a reservoir of goodwill toward America exist among a majority of Iranians. The people of Iran would welcome America's principled, transparent and vocal support of the movement for democracy and rule-of-law in their country. Therefore, U.S. policy should not be held hostage to the history of U.S.-Iranian relations and events surrounding 1953. As far as a majority of freedom-loving Iranians are concerned, 1953 is history. Washington must overcome this ingrained psychological barrier, created in large measure by U.S. and Iranian academics of the left and self-loathing businessmen and journalists dependent upon Iranian visas and access (see section on U.S.-Iranian ties).

4. Irrespective of who is President of Iran, the Islamic Republic's constitution specifically rejects popular sovereignty and puts ultimate power in the hands of the Supreme Leader, un-elected by the people and answerable only to "Allah."

5. The popular overthrow of the Islamic Republic of Iran will send a very powerful message to the entire Muslim world—Islam does not solve the socio-economic problems that are at their root internal: poverty and corruption, suppression, absence of democracy, and economic opportunity.

Public Opinion in Iran.

In August of 2002, the Tarrance Group conducted a poll of public opinion in Tehran. This research project— the first of its kind—was designed to fulfill two main objectives: a) provide a broad assessment of the social, economic, and political landscape of Iran; and b) determine whether or not Iranians believe in a fundamental change of the political system in Iran.

The findings from this survey validate stories that have recently been reported by international news agencies about a growing level of dissatisfaction within Iran towards the current regime. One finding in particular best summarizes the current mood in Iran: 63 percent of respondents believe that freedom and economic opportunity can only come as a result of "a fundamental change" in Iran's system of government. Agreement with this viewpoint exceeds 50 percent among every major demographic group and is highest among those who rely on satellite television and the internet for information about issues facing Iran (72 percent and 75 percent respectively).

Along the same line, 71 percent of respondents indicate that they would support a national referendum that allows the people of Iran to decide what system of government is best for the country. Once again, this is something that transcends all demographic categories.

The mounting frustration within Iran's citizenry can partially be attributed to the facts that only one-in-three respondents (33 percent) feel that Khatami has delivered on his campaign promises, and there is little expectation that things will change during his remaining 3 years in office. While 29 percent of respondents say

Khatami is capable of bringing reform, a plurality (41 percent) of Iranians believe that it is time for a new approach.

The maximum support the regime gets is between 15 to 19 percent. The cross tabs indicate that this level of support is from respondents whose families have clerical ties.

In what comes as a rejection of the regime's 23 years of hostility against the exiled Iranian community, 72 percent of those surveyed would welcome the involvement of Iranians living abroad in helping to rebuild their homeland. Moreover, just one-in-four respondents (25 percent) are of the opinion that history will judge the "founder of modern Iran" unfavorably; a finding that essentially means that the Pahlavi era is well regarded by many despite the regime's attempt to convince people otherwise.

In conclusion, the majority of Iranians living in Tehran want to see fundamental changes in the way their country is governed. People feel that the clerics have gone too far and overstepped their traditional role, and that the country would be better served if they were not directly in charge of the government. Part of the solution—as supported by a decisive majority of survey respondents—is to hold a "free, fair, and transparent national referendum," allowing the people of Iran to select the system of government that they desire.

History of U.S.-Iranian Relations.

Much of the policymaking community in Washington has held back from making aggressive policy recommendations towards the clerical regime. This is the result of a complete misreading of the broad outlines of our country's relations with Iran. The United States has nothing to apologize for concerning its relations with Iran. In fact, America's timely interventions preserved Iran's territorial integrity and prevented that country from falling behind the "Iron Curtain."

President Bush should begin his assessment of U.S.-Iranian policy with an objective look at the history of relations between Washington and Tehran. By gaining a historical perspective on U.S.-Iranian relations, President Bush would understand that while officials of the Islamic regime have been lecturing America on what Washington has done wrong, the United States was not always seen as an enemy of Iran's national interests.

America's first attempt at helping Iran was in 1911, when London and St. Petersburg were manipulating the debt-ridden Qajar dynasty. Morgan Shuster, an official of the U.S. Treasury Department, was appointed financial advisor by the Iranian government to prevent the strangling of an impoverished Iran by Britain and Russia. Unfortunately, Britain and Russia succeeded in sabotaging his mission.

In 1925, after a bloodless coup supported by the military, Reza Shah Pahlavi assumed the throne and embarked on the modernization of Iran with the help of American advisors. This attempt to bring Iran into the 20th century ended with the onset of World War II.

In 1941, Soviet troops reoccupied northern Iran, once again threatening its sovereignty. From 1941 to 1946, the Soviet Union, with the support of the KGB-infiltrated Iranian communist party, began to dismember Iran by creating a second "Republic of Azerbaijan" on the Iranian side of the border. When the war ended, Soviet troops refused to leave northern Iran. Iran then appealed to the United Nations, and America forcefully supported Iran's right to independence. Meanwhile, George Allen, then American ambassador to Iran and an ardent supporter of its autonomy, was arguing for more direct American assistance. The result was an ultimatum from President Harry S Truman to Josef Stalin to get out of Iran. The Soviets withdrew, and Iran was saved from disappearing behind the Iron Curtain.

During his CNN debut, Iran's President Mohammad Khatami focused on the 1953 coup against Prime Minister Mohammad Mossadeq. Khatami charged that the ousting of Mossadeq and the Shah's return to power with Washington's assistance was a major contaminator of U.S.-Iranian relations. The truth is more complex. Until 1953, the United States had supported Mossadeq, particularly when Britain attempted to remove him because he was viewed as a threat to British oil interests in Iran. By 1953, however, Mossadeq's policies had brought Iran to the brink of financial ruin. Iran's communist party—already strong among the industrial working class, intellectuals, students, and army officers—further extended its influence during this period. The Soviet flag and Stalin's pictures appeared in the streets of Tehran. Concerns about the communist threat to Iran forced America to act against Mossadeq's increasingly authoritarian tactics and in favor of the Shah. Once again, America's timely intervention—which, ironically, was supported by the clerics at the time due to their dislike of atheistic communism—saved Iran from falling under Soviet domination.

The one episode in this long history that stands out as a policy mistake occurred in 1964, when the U.S. Department of Defense pushed for, and got, full immunity from prosecution for all American personnel stationed in Iran. Iranians, irrespective of their political ideology, were outraged. This policy mistake gave an unknown cleric named Ruhollah Khomeini a national issue on which to rise to power: "They have reduced the Iranian people to a level lower than that of a dog." On November 4, 1964, Khomeini was exiled from Iran for his remarks, and on the same day 15 years later, he sanctioned the attack on the American embassy.

During the 1970s, Washington's military alliance with Tehran was a major deterrent to Saddam Hussein's designs on Iran and the Persian Gulf. This mutually beneficial alliance came to an abrupt end with the establishment of the Islamic Republic of Iran and its rejection of so many things American. Emboldened by the sudden disappearance of the Shah, Hussein invaded Iran in 1980. The people of Iran paid dearly for their government's anti-American policy—one million died, and millions more were wounded.

The taking of 52 American diplomats hostage by Iranian students in 1979 and the subsequent Algiers Agreement that ended this hostage crisis in 1980, is used by some within the policymaking community as a basis for refraining from adopting a policy of regime change. The Algiers Agreement calls for "noninterference" by Washington in the internal affairs of Iran. It is the opinion of this writer that Iranian-sponsored acts of terrorism against the United States overseas render this document's clause pertaining to "noninterference" as null and void. Furthermore, America's national security paradigm has changed significantly since the tragedy of September 11, 2001. We cannot allow any rogue nation, including Islamic Iran, to develop a nuclear bomb and blackmail and/or threaten the United States and our allies in the region.

With this long history in mind, the United States should not invest its diplomatic and political energies in apologizing for recent "past mistakes" in exchange for normalization of relations with Tehran, or refrain from adopting a more robust policy towards those responsible for the murder of Americans. Instead, Washington must take the high moral ground and lend its unwavering support to empowering the people of Iran for a regime change.

Implications of Regime Change.

The geopolitical and economic consequences of a regime change in Iran and an end to that country's pursuit of a nuclear bomb are as follows.

- The cornerstone of U.S. policy in the Persian Gulf is the uninterrupted exploration, development, and transportation of oil and gas to international markets. A regime change in Iran would significantly enhance this long-standing U.S. policy.

- Enhance the stability and security of Washington's Persian Gulf allies. Countries like Bahrain, Qatar, the United Arab Emirates (UAE), and Kuwait would breath easier knowing that the geopolitical vacuum created by the fall of Saddam Hussein would not be filled by Islamic Iran. Bahrain would feel less threatened knowing that Islamic Iran would not manipulate and encourage the Shi'a of Bahrain to challenge King Hamad's reforms. The Amir of Qatar would not have to worry about a nuclear accident threatening the massive liquified natural gas (LNG) infrastructure built to market natural gas to markets worldwide. The United Arab Emirates (UAE) might finally find a receptive government in Tehran willing to compromise on the three disputed islands of Abu Musa and the Bigger and Lesser Tombs.

- Decouple Russia from its military, diplomatic, and geopolitical ally in Tehran. The new Iranian government would have very little justification for pursuing a relationship with the Russian

Federation and, in fact, might view its relations with Russia through a new competitive context; namely, competing with Russia for pursuit of customers in the worldwide natural gas markets.

- The nascent government of Afghanistan would no longer have to be concerned over Iranian adventurism within its borders. This would increase the chances for stability and economic reconstruction in Afghanistan. A Kabul-Tehran axis defined by cooperation and alliance with the United States could only enhance stability in that part of the world and rout out remaining elements of al-Qaeda and Taliban.

- Images of millions of Iranians marching through the streets of Iran chanting "Death to the Islamic Republic" broadcast across the Muslim world would be nothing less than a historic earthquake of enormous proportion. The rejection of Islam as a form of governance would impact Iran's neighbors Turkey, Pakistan, Afghanistan, and Iraq immediately. The question that would be asked throughout the Muslim world would be "Why, why have Iranians rejected Islam?" Pakistan's increasingly radicalized Islamic politics, Turkey's new Islamic Party, the Shi'a of Lebanon, Bahrain, Iraq, and Saudi Arabia and Egypt's underground Islamic cells would all be impacted.

- Regime change in Iran would put an immediate end to support for Hamas, Hezbollah, Islamic Jihad, al-Qaeda, and the Popular Front for the Liberation of Palestine-General Command (PFLP-GC). The new Iran would cut off all ties to these terrorist organizations out of principle but more importantly out of economic necessity. Iran's meager resources would be devoted to rebuilding Iran.

- The first diplomatic act of a new, secular, and free Iran would be to recognize Israel's right to exist. Throwing Iran's diplomatic weight behind Israel would further isolate the Arab world and its intransigence towards Israel.

- An Iran that is focused on developing its vast oil and gas resources in the Persian Gulf would allow for a more rational exploitation of the Caspian Sea hydrocarbon resources. A pro-American Iran willing to act as a stable corridor would add multiple pipeline options for the transport of Caspian Sea oil and gas to international markets.

- Beyond geopolitical considerations, President Bush should indicate to the Iranian people that America is ready once again to be Iran's partner in prosperity. Both sides would have much to gain. Iran's more than 70 million people would once again constitute a market for American goods and services. American energy companies would have the chance to invest in Iran's vast hydrocarbon resources. In short, economic engagement can lay the foundations for a return to normalcy in U.S.-Iran relations.

What Needs to be Done.

Within Iran, the youth that make up a majority of the population, journalists of reformist newspapers, clerics who question the legitimacy of the Supreme Leader, and women who are at the forefront of defying the ruling theocrats are Washington's natural allies. Engagement and collaboration between these groups and America should be the cornerstone of U.S. policy towards Iran.

However, a fundamental problem facing U.S. policy towards Iran is the lack of available resources to fund projects in support of freedom and democracy in Iran. As a result, a significant vacuum exists in U.S. policy towards Iran that is unfortunately being filled by apologists for the Islamic Republic of Iran in the United States. The cost of empowering the Iranian people to change their regime (over a 2-year timetable) should not exceed $200 million. (Note: The Department of Defense (DoD) spends $3.6 billion/month on operations in Iraq and $700 million/month on operations in Afghanistan.)

Adequate funding of projects that are inline with the broader U.S. policy objectives outlined by President Bush's State of the Union

Addresses can go a long way towards empowering the people of Iran to affect change in their country.

The following are some funding options for review and consideration by the U.S. DoD:

- Short-term Funding:

    o Produce and disseminate a civil disobedience training video via satellite into Iran. This Farsi language video with young men and women as instructors would highlight the role of civil disobedience in toppling dictatorships. The video would then be distributed throughout Iran.

    o Hold a major conference on Iran at Georgetown University. Very senior U.S. Government officials and leading Iranian opposition figures would attend this conference. The conference would be broadcast live into Iran with the purpose of demonstrating to those inside Iran that the disparate opposition is united in its demand for a regime change. Images of a united opposition at a conference with senior officials from the Bush Administration broadcast live into Iran (and carried by all U.S. and non-U.S. outlets) would be a major boost to the morale of those inside Iran willing to confront the security forces of the regime. It would also send a very powerful message to members of the ruling clergy that their days may be numbered.

    o Produce and disseminate educational videos in Farsi on democracy in America to the Farsi-speaking media for broadcast into Iran. A major component of this project would be to highlight the positive role that American women of Iranian descent are playing in the life of our country. At this juncture in Iran's history, it is very important to highlight the failures of the regime and to contrast this with the realities of life in America through the lens of the American-Iranian community.

    o Investigate, compile, and disseminate the human rights abuses of the regime through visits by the victims of these human rights violations to Western capitals. In addition to the fundamental differences with the Islamic regime on such issues as weapons of mass destruction (WMD) and terrorism, it is important that the issue of human rights be a major focus of American demands for the Iranian people.

o   Invite senior and junior Shia clergy from Tehran, Qoma, and Mashad to the United States for meetings with their Jewish, Christian, and Muslim counterparts.

o   Sponsor a trip for 30 Iranian journalists to take a tour called "Get to Know America and Americans." Let them then go back to Iran asking this fundamental question: "Why do Americans of Iranian descent living in the United States enjoy a higher standard of living than Iranians in Iran?"

o   Invite leaders of the student movement to testify on Capitol Hill about their ordeal and how they envision a future Iran. Giving these young men and women a platform would provide enormous moral support to the entire movement inside the country.

o   Invite prominent Iranian women to meet with female members of Congress, successful entrepreneurs, journalists, and nonprofit organizations like Mothers Against Drunk Driving (MADD).

o   Immediately fund satellite TV stations based in Los Angeles that are viewed by millions inside Iran. Integration of these stations into a National Iranian Radio and Television Network would provide an excellent platform for U.S. officials to enunciate their vision for U.S.-Iranian relations and for Iranian dissidents to share their vision of a future Iran with their compatriots.

- Long-term Funding:

  o Fund for 1 year the operating expenses of a U.S.-based nonprofit foundation established to support democratic principles, secularism, human rights, and a free market economy in Iran. This 1-year funding would cover personnel and major stand-alone projects. All the projects outlined above could be rolled into the activities of this U.S.-based nonprofit foundation.

  o Provide funding to produce a comprehensive blueprint for a post-theocratic Iran. This blueprint would cover the future shape of Iran's polity in the following areas: constitution, foreign and national security, energy, agriculture, health care, finance, commerce, role of religion in society, and economics. The blueprint would be disseminated into Iran through an aggressive media campaign to demonstrate to the Iranian people, "A Vision Of The Future Beyond An Islamic Republic."

These major initiatives could be launched at a Rose Garden event where President Bush announces via satellite to the Iranian people (carried by Radio Farda, Voice of America, British Broadcasting Corporation, Radio Israel, etc.) his firm commitment and dedication to empowering the Iranian people to change their form of government. Prominent members of the President's own American-Iranian staff, prominent and not-so-prominent members of the American-Iranian community, and members of the Iran National Coalition would be present at this event. This historic occasion would mark the beginning of the end for the Islamic Republic of Iran and embolden the Iranian people to rise.

Iranian Dissidents and a National Coalition.

One of the only prominent Iranian opposition figures outside Iran publicly calling for an end to Iran's pursuit of a nuclear bomb is Reza Pahlavi. In both his public and private speeches he has staked out a position in line with U.S. concerns about regional instability as a result of nuclear proliferation. In addition, and according to various press reports, his message of civil disobedience, nonviolence, and national referendum are gaining momentum inside Iran, albeit at a slow pace.

The rationale for supporting Reza Pahlavi and other dissidents outside Iran (like Dr. Azar Nafisi, Dr. Manouchehr Gandji, Mehmat Ali Chehregani, Sepehr Zanganeh, Ladan Boroumand, Mehangiz Kar, Parviz Sayyad, Abbas Goli Bakhtiar, Esmail Khoee, and Hamid Ladjevardi) is that there is a limit to how far one can criticize the regime while inside Iran. It is only from the outside that one can seriously question and challenge the regime. It is therefore imperative that the United States encourage and support the activities of these dissidents as symbols of opposition to the Islamic Regime. However, the United States must not impose a solution that includes dissidents like Reza Pahlavi. Rather, the United States must encourage the formation of an Iranian National Coalition with Reza Pahlavi and other dissidents as members of the coalition.

Critics of this approach will argue that this is a repeat of America's 1953 debacle in Iran. This argument is far from accurate. The United States would merely be leveling the playing field for Reza Pahlavi and members of the Iranian National Coalition to put forward their ideas as to how Iran's future should be shaped. The Iranian people would make the final decision in a free, fair, and transparent referendum.

In order to ensure the success of Iranian dissidents and the Iranian National Coalition, the following steps need to be taken:

1. Provide logistical support for the direct broadcast of dissidents' messages into Iran.

2. Give more airtime to members of the Iranian National Coalition on the VOA, Radio Farda, and other U.S.-based and non-U.S.-based outlets.

3. Identify "safe houses" in the United States, Europe, and the Middle East for members of the regime who wish to meet with Reza Pahlavi and members of the coalition.

4. Invite Reza Pahlavi and members of the coalition to Capitol Hill to testify and share visions for Iran with the U.S. Congress.

5. Ask America's allies in the Persian Gulf to fully fund the activities of Reza Pahlavi and the Iranian National Coalition for a 2-year period.

Iran Coordinator.

The activities outlined above can be supervised under the Office of Iran Coordinator. President Bush should appoint an Iran Coordinator in order to ensure an outcome favorable to U.S. interests in the post-theocratic Iran. The people of Iran are now looking beyond the Islamic regime, and President Bush's recent statements since September 11 have emboldened them and inspired the more courageous to publicly challenge that regime. An Iran Coordinator is needed to ensure that President Bush's intentions are communicated to Iranians in an honest and unadulterated fashion. The Iran Coordinator would also engage the people of Iran in a clear and open dialogue about their future.

Further, the role of an Iran Coordinator would include providing the administration with timely, pro-active policy initiatives designed to ensure that the government of Iran does not sabotage U.S. efforts in post-Saddam Hussein Iraq. The campaign to liberate Iraq from Saddam Hussein dovetails with Washington's goal of exporting democracy to Iran. Any U.S. policy toward Iraq and Iran must be mutually reinforcing in order to achieve maximum benefits for U.S. national security interests. Therefore, it would be important that the Iran Coordinator explain America's Iraq policy to the Iranian people via the VOA, BBC, Radio Israel, Radio Free Iran and other satellite stations based in Los Angeles.

Appointment of an Iran Coordinator would be one of the most significant demonstrations of America's resolve to establish relations with the democratic and free Iran of the future. It would demonstrate that the United States is serious when it says that it will support the people of Iran in their quest for freedom and democracy. Indeed, the Islamic regime could well begin to unravel immediately after this appointment was announced because of the psychological effect on the mind-set of all Iranians.

A fundamental feature of Iranian political culture has been the "Green Light Syndrome." In other words, the West in general, and Washington in particular, decide the course of events in countries like Iran. Therefore, if and when the time comes for one regime to go or for a person to be supported, the United States will give the Green Light, and it will happen. The majority of Iranians already view President Bush's "Axis of Evil" speech and his recent strong statement in support of the people as a sign that Washington is ready to give that "green light." The appointment of an Iran coordinator would be further "evidence" that the United States has given the "green light" that the regime must go.

The Coordinator would report to the National Security Advisor and attend all policy sessions on Iran. The purpose of the Iran Coordinator would be to ensure that any regime change in Iran is favorable to U.S. interests. The primary responsibility of the Iran Coordinator would be to disseminate the administration's policy into Iran and to advise the administration of the Iranian response. To this end, the Coordinator would vet opposition groups to ensure that they share Washington's national security interests and are genuine democrats. Finally, maximum impact would be achieved if the Iran Coordinator were fluent in Farsi and Azeri, understood Iranian political culture, and was an American of Iranian descent.

Islamic Bomb versus Iranian Bomb.

A fundamental dynamic at play in Iran today is a renewed sense of national pride at being Iranian. Islam, both as a religion and form of governance, has taken a backseat to nationalism. The historic struggle between traditionalism and modernity that has been the mainstay of Iranian history is now swinging away from traditionalism. Indeed, the Islamic Revolution of 1979 was, in many ways, a counter-revolution. After years of taking a backseat to modernity, the forces of traditionalism had finally triumphed. In many respects, Mohammad Khatami's first victory in 1997, owed as much to his use of nationalist themes and the inclusion of pride at being Iranian as well as a Muslim nation.

Viewed in this context, any announcement by the Islamic Republic of Iran that Iran successfully detonated a nuclear bomb would be welcomed by an overwhelming majority of the people. This euphoria would be temporary but nonetheless widespread because it would appeal to the Iranian sense of nationalism. Should the regime make an announcement that the "nation has acquired an Iranian bomb" then it would be welcome and legitimize the regime. However, should the regime portray this event as an Islamic bomb at the service of the Muslim world, then the entire context of what this means to the nation would change. An "Islamic bomb" would be viewed by the Iranians as a tool in the hands of the clergy to intimidate and blackmail its neighbors. An Iranian bomb would be viewed as a legitimate means to defend the nation against any real or perceived enemy. It would be justified as: "Well, if the Pakistanis have it, why not us. If the Israelis have it, why not us. If the Americans have it, why not us."

The Clerics and a Nuclear Bomb.

The 14 grand ayatollahs living in Iran would most likely support and give their blessing to the continuation of Iran's pursuit of a nuclear bomb so long as it was put into the service of Islam; a defense of Muslims and not used for offensive purposes. Of the 5,000 recognized ayatollahs in Iran, some might disagree with resources being diverted to pursuing a nuclear option, but a majority would be supportive. Those clerics opposed to the regime such as Grand Ayatollah Montazeri would not welcome the news of a bomb in the hands of the regime, but he would be supportive of the fact that the "Muslim nation of Iran has acquired this capability."

Junior clerics who have been vocal in their opposition to the concept of velayate-faqih, such as Mohsen Kadivar and Abdollah Nouri, would in all likelihood support continuation of Iran's quest for a nuclear bomb. They would, however, lend their support so long as the program was transparent, in order to ease the country out of its current international isolation. They would, for example, favor open access to all facilities.

Nonclerics and a Nuclear Bomb.

The relatives of the powerful such as Mohammad-Reza Khatami; Jamileh Kadivar, the wife of Ataollah Mohajerani, Khatami's former Minister of Islamic Guidance; Ali-Reza Nouri, the younger brother of Abdollah Nouri; and Hadi Khamenei, the estranged brother of the Supreme Leader, would also welcome Iran's quest for a nuclear bomb. This group, would, however, view this weapon in the broader context of Iranian deterrence capabilities and not within the Islamic context.

Gholam-Hossein Karbaschi, the former mayor of Tehran, may play a prominent role in the future of Iran and, as such, his position on the issue of Iran's quest for a nuclear bomb would be instructive. As Tehran's no-nonsense mayor, Karbaschi turned Tehran into a city "that works." His tenure as mayor and popularity during this period, coupled with his still close ties to former President Rafsanjani, suggests that he would pursue the nuclear option. He would see this as a political platform for his own advancement, albeit using the bomb itself in the context of defending Iran.

Any members of the regime's revolutionary security forces that emerged to take charge in a coup or regime change scenario would most likely continue the quest for a nuclear bomb. They most likely would see this as a positive platform and a nationalist agenda that would play well with the majority of Iranians. Furthermore, as a "military person" the issue would be put into the context of Iran's need to deter its "regional enemies" or stay at a parity with its neighbors, Pakistan and India.

Conclusion.

The United States has a historic opportunity to put the genie of Islamic fundamentalism back into the bottle by empowering the Iranian people to change their regime. If Washington is serious about ending Islamic Iran's nuclear ambitions; if Washington is serious about ending Islamic Iran's support for global terrorism; if Washington is serious about promoting democratic pluralism in the Middle East; then a robust proactive policy of regime change is the only option to consider. In the end, America must remain true to the core values that have made our country a beacon of hope for millions around the world: freedom, rule-of-law, and economic opportunity. It is time we made it very clear to the Iranian people that we support their quest for freedom and will act upon this quest, and that we will not engage their tormentors in any way shape or form. Empowering the people of Iran to change their regime is in America's national security interests; but it is also a long-standing tradition of our moral fabric as a nation. The words of another President are instructive in this regard:

> Whenever the standard of freedom has been and shall be unfurled, there will be America's heart, her benediction and her prayers.
>
> John Quincy Adams

CHAPTER 5

WINNING IRANIAN HEARTS AND MINDS

Abbas William Samii*

Iran could become a nuclear capable state in the next 24-30 months (June 2003-December 2005), in light of progress at Bushehr and other, undeclared, facilities. The military option—from preemptive strikes against nuclear facilities to a full-scale invasion—is one way to preclude this eventuality. Many Iranians have a positive impression of the United States and a dislike of their own regime, but it is very unlikely that they would react positively to an American attack or to an American-backed successor government.

Iranian attitudes towards the U.S. currently fall between two extremes. Iran and its people can seem rabidly anti-American, with a history of hostage takings and mobs continuing to chant "Death to America" on a weekly basis. American visitors to the country, however, report that such activities are almost *pro forma* by now, and a 2002 opinion poll in Tehran found that almost three-quarters of the population favors the resumption of direct Iran-U.S. talks. (The United States broke relations with Iran on April 7, 1980.) At the same time, visitors to Iran describe a proud and nationalistic people who retain skepticism about U.S. motives, and opinion polls reflect this.

The United States could mitigate the impact of any military action against Iran by persuading Iranians beforehand of its positive intentions towards them, and this will take more than White House declarations of support for the Iranian people. This chapter recommends several concrete actions to win Iranians' hearts and minds. Washington should provide disaster relief to Iran, permit enhanced international cooperation in Iranian counternarcotics activities, assist Iranian HIV/AIDS prevention and treatment

*Dr. Samii is the Regional Analysis Coordinator for Southwest Asia at Radio Free Europe/Radio Liberty, Inc. (RFE/RL). The views expressed here do not necessarily reflect the official policy or position of RFE/RL.

programs, and provide assistance to Iranian refugee support activities. Washington also should encourage Iranian participation in multilateral international fora and acknowledge Iran's concerns about regional developments, ease restrictions on Iranians' ability to visit the United States, and end its resistance to Iranian membership in the World Trade Organization.

All of these actions would be pointless if Iranians are not aware of them. Coupled with the concrete steps of the hearts and minds campaign, therefore, must be an aggressive information operations campaign that would counter Tehran's anti-American propaganda and disinformation. Accurate information about U.S. activities should be relayed to Iran via FM and shortwave radio, satellite television, and the Internet.

The policy recommendations in this chapter may not have a serious short-term effect because most foreign-policy decisionmaking in Iran is in the hands of a small elite. The impact of a hearts and minds campaign would be much more significant in a decade, as the 44.3 million Iranians who are under 30—roughly two-thirds of the population of 66.4 million—and who did not participate in such formative experiences as life under the pro-U.S. monarchy, activism in the 1978-79 revolution, or fighting in the 1980-88 Iran-Iraq War, come of age.[1]

PUBLIC PERCEPTIONS AND THE GREAT SATAN

It is unrealistic to be very specific about the attitudes of a population as large as Iran's, but for many observers, a number of images stand out—blindfolded American diplomats being led out of the Embassy in Tehran in 1979 and a cleric toying with the remains of an American serviceman killed in the April 1980 hostage rescue mission, burning of the American flag at public events, and Friday prayer congregations chanting "Death to America." Then there is the description of the United States as "the Great Satan."[2]

The Satanic reference to the United States was more than just a comparison to the Devil. It was an "important device in the reeducation of the Iranian people to the new revolutionary ideology of the Iranian state"—a lamentation that materialism had replaced spiritualism and the assignment of blame to the United States.[3] The

Great Satan drew men from the path of righteousness towards sin. The Iranian monarch, his family, and his entourage were corrupt, but the United States was perceived as "the ultimate source of that corruption."[4] Moreover, Iran-U.S. relations were marred by misperceptions and misunderstanding.

The Great Satan terminology also reflected "outrage" directed against the United States. A scholar explained:

> The outrage felt by the Iranian people was heightened by the knowledge, rarely admitted after the revolution, that many Iranians were themselves largely to blame for Iran's economic and social difficulties during the years of Pahlavi rule.[5]

Some Iranians may chant against the Great Satan, but according to visitors, the Iranian public does not share the anti-American sentiments of its leadership. Journalist Elaine Sciolino developed a set of rules to help her "survive the setbacks and embrace the surprises of Iran," and rule number 12 is, "Iranians Like Americans."[6] She notes that Iran officially sees America as its greatest enemy, but at the same time, many Iranians see America as the Promised Land. Sciolino cites the popularity of inexpensive pirated software, CDs, and videos, the availability of knock-off Wrangler jeans in Qom, and the way in which individuals who demonstrated against America would ask her for help getting a visa. Throughout her book, furthermore, Sciolino notes that she is generally received with great warmth.

Two of Sciolino's other rules, however, lead one to question this warmth. One rule is, "Hospitality Doesn't Mean Openness," and the other rule is, "Being Polite is Better than Telling the Truth."[7] These rules result in reservations about the depth of fondness for Americans that Sciolino describes.

Journalist Afshin Molavi has written about Iranians and their attitudes towards the United States, too. Molavi writes that as he is sitting in a park with the Friday Prayer sermon blasting anti-American vituperative in the background, a group of young women approaches him; one asks for help in completing a Green Card application and another describes her application to an American university.[8] In another case, Molavi is watching a hard-liner rally against the writers of an allegedly blasphemous play.[9] The crowd is led in cries of "The Playwrights Must Die," "Reform Means Blasphemy," "Death to Israel," and, of course, "Death to America." After the rally, however, one of the more enthusiastic chanters approaches Molavi and asks, "How can I get a Green Card?"

Like Sciolino, Molavi recognizes that Iranians are sometimes economical with the truth and may not be completely forthcoming about their real feelings; in his words, "a remarkable ability to be evasive, tell half-truths, and lie outright."[10] He describes this as a survival mechanism. And the quest for Green Cards appears to be associated with the quest for better economic opportunities and greater social freedom. Indeed, many younger Iranians travel to Damascus to get Canadian visas for these very reasons and because American visas are relatively difficult to get.

Another American reporter who has traveled to Iran extensively since the Islamic revolution, Robin Wright, also notes the dichotomy of opinions towards the United States. In 1982 she encountered a group of Revolutionary Guards who were looking for Americans; when she reluctantly identified herself they wanted to know the score of the Nebraska-Oklahoma football game.[11] She also notes that thousands of Iranians, including some top government officials, were educated in the United States, and she describes the annual reunion of the Islamic Association of U.S. and Canadian Graduates.[12] Youthful participants at the annual rally to commemorate the seizure of the U.S. Embassy are bused in, and one tells Wright that he sees it as a day off from school, while many others say that if given a choice, they would rather watch an American movie.[13] At the same rally, a young man asks Wright for help getting a visa to the United States.

Polls and surveys have been used in recent years to weigh public opinion. Iran's Ministry of Islamic Culture and Guidance sponsored a series of polls in 2001 that used innovative means to explore Iranians' sentiments on a range of issues (but not on attitudes towards other countries).[14] Some 16,274 people in 28 cities participated in the polling, but it does not appear that such thoroughness is the norm.

The Ayandeh Research Institute and the Islamic Culture and Guidance Ministry's National Institute for Research Studies and Opinion Polls conducted a survey in September 2002 which found that 74.7 percent of Tehran residents favored negotiations with the United States, and 64.5 percent favored the resumption of Iran-U.S. talks.[15] Yet 70.4 percent of respondents said that the United States is unreliable, 62 percent did not believe in Washington's sincerity in the anti-terrorism campaign, and 65.6 percent did not think that Washington is sincere in its defense of freedom and democracy.

Two later surveys provided contradictory results. A late-March 2003 telephone poll of Tehran residents found that 84 percent of respondents believe that Iran should continue its current policy of neutrality and noncooperation with the United States.[16] A survey conducted 3 weeks later found that 83 percent of Tehran citizens distrust the U.S. Government, and 85 percent of those polled think of the United States as an "invading and colonial country."[17]

This reversal in attitudes towards the United States can be explained in several ways. The latter two surveys were conducted when U.S. forces were participating in Operation IRAQI FREEDOM (which started on March 20, 2003), and most Iranian newspapers were not published from March 20-April 5, due to the Noruz (the Iranian new year) holiday. During this period the only readily available sources of information were Iranian radio and television, which produced highly critical, biased, and inaccurate reports about the war. *Entekhab, Iran, Aftab-i Yazd,* and *Yas-i No* newspapers produced a few special issues during this period, but these, too, were generally critical of the war effort and played up the negative aspects of the conflict. Although the survey results were made available, furthermore, information on the sample size or survey technique was not reported.

There are questions about the September 2002 survey, too. During the pollsters' trial, the public prosecutor charged some of the defendants with forging the poll's results, completing questionnaires without questioning anybody, not actually visiting some of the addresses that they listed, and sometimes listing addresses that did not exist.[18] Needless to say, being charged with a crime does not make a person guilty, nor can one view the trial relating to the poll as much more than a political event.

Iranians are friendly towards Americans and favorably inclined towards the United States, but they are also nationalistic and favor their independence. These sentiments are to some extent rooted in the country's history of encounters with foreign invaders and neo-colonialists. Therefore, President George W. Bush's inclusion of Iran in his January 2002 "axis of evil" reference was insulting to many Iranians, although the Iranian legislature later questioned the Defense Minister about activities that contributed to this statement. "Iranians' fierce nationalism is characterized by intense suspicion and outright resentment of outside influences," a former Iranian official writes, and he warns, "any U.S. strategy that even remotely raises the specter of foreign interference in Iran is doomed to fail."[19]

POLICY RECOMMENDATIONS

The United States can enact several measures that would build on the pre-existing positive sentiments described above. The ones listed below would have negligible costs for the United States. These policy recommendations could be enacted immediately, but it would take some time for them to have an impact.

Disaster Relief.

The United States should continue to provide disaster relief for Iran. The U.S. Agency for International Development (USAID) in March 1997 provided $25,000 to the International Federation of the Red Cross to assist victims of Ardabil Province earthquakes that killed almost 1,000 people, injured 2,600, and left more than 60,000 people homeless.[20]

The United States also provided assistance in May 1997 after an earthquake measuring 7.1 on the Richter scale caused devastation in Khorasan Province. In June 2002 an earthquake measuring 6.3 on the Richter scale killed more than 230 people, injured another 1,300, and left an estimated 25,000 people homeless. USAID sent $350,000 worth of humanitarian aid (water containers, water purification systems, blankets, and personal hygiene kits) to Iran via a chartered aircraft, and provided another $50,000 to International Federation of the Red Cross and Red Crescent Societies to provide blankets to the victims.[21]

Iran's Sistan va Baluchistan Province is badly affected by

drought, and the main source of water there is the Helmand River, which originates in Afghanistan. The Taliban essentially blocked the river's flow into Iran, and, although the situation improved in Autumn 2002 due the improved relationship between Tehran and Kabul, Iranians continue to bemoan the relative scarcity of water. The United States could encourage Kabul to be more generous with the river's waters.

Counternarcotics Cooperation.[22]

Tehran claims that up to 2 million Iranians are addicted to or abuse drugs, and drug-related convictions account for 40 percent of the prison population. American nongovernmental organizations already have provided assistance for addiction treatment and counseling. Washington could underwrite such activities. Moreover, club drugs such as ecstasy (MDMA) are becoming popular in Iran, and the United States could share its experiences in dealing with this new phenomenon.

Most of the drugs come from Afghanistan, the world's largest opium producer, and Tehran's main way of dealing with this problem is interdiction—static defenses, law enforcement, and military measures. Tehran has promoted crop substitution in Afghanistan and is providing counternarcotics training for its neighbors, and these are areas in which Iran and the United States could cooperate. The UN Office for Drugs and Crime (UNODC, previously the UN Drug Control Program) has an office in Tehran and is actively involved with Iran's Drug Control Headquarters. U.S. legislation (the Foreign Assistance Act of 1961, see below), namely the requirement that the United States reduce its contribution to an international program in a proportionate share to its contribution to Iran, can and should be waived in order to facilitate such cooperation.

HIV/AIDS Prevention and Treatment.

The first case of AIDS in Iran was reported in 1987. Some 4,846 people in Iran have been diagnosed as HIV-positive as of mid-2003, although there are unofficial estimates that up to 23,000 people in the country have AIDS.[23] Iran's problem with narcotics is the main reason for the prevalence of the virus, with the sharing of contaminated needles, especially in prisons, accounting for 65 percent of the cases. So far, the main Iranian solution to this problem has been to separate addicted prisoners from those who are jailed for narcotics offenses.[24]

Iran's wider approach focuses mainly on prevention through the provision of information and educational materials to patients and the community; voluntary testing and counseling; serological and behavioral surveillance; and HIV care, support, and treatment. Moreover, related medicine is distributed free of charge. The World Health Organization (WHO) provides support to the Iranian Ministry of Health, Treatment, and Medical Education's program to control HIV/AIDS. This program includes blood screening, health promotion and education, training workshops; and developing local capacities, expertise, and awareness among public health workers. Washington could facilitate public health professionals' travel to Iran to participate in intellectual exchanges, and it could make more money available for the WHO activities.

Refugee Assistance.

Iran currently hosts some 2.55 million refugees—2,355,000 Afghans, 203,000 Iraqis, and 5,522 others. The government, which is facing an estimated 25 percent unemployment rate, has enacted a number of policies to encourage the refugees to go home because they supposedly take jobs that would otherwise go to Iranians, they consume social services, and they supposedly contribute to the crime rate. These measures include forcible repatriation, the withdrawal of services (ex: children's education, health care), and the refusal to permit Afghan husbands of Iranian women to stay in Iran. Employers who hire refugees who do not have a work permit face heavy fines.

The United States could provide assistance to Iranian refugee support activities through the Office of the UN High Commissioner for Refugees (UNHCR). Not only would this help the refugees, but also it would ease the pressure on the Transitional Administration of Afghanistan and on the fledgling Iraqi leadership. Indeed, in 2000 the United States provided the UNHCR with $7.4 million to support its activities on behalf of Afghan refugees in Iran and Pakistan, and it provided a nongovernmental organization called the International Rescue Committee with $905,349 to assist repatriation of Afghan refugees from Iran and Pakistan.

Multilateral Dialogue.

The encouragement of Iranian participation in multilateral international fora and acknowledgement of Iranian concerns in bilateral meetings has taken place before and should continue. The most recent example is the meeting of American and Iranian officials to discuss the war in Iraq.[25] Tehran has been praised for its role in the November 2001 meeting in Bonn, Switzerland, about Afghanistan, and it was seen as an important participant in the UN's 6+2 grouping (Afghanistan's immediate neighbors, the United States, and Russia).

Iran first offered to mediate between Armenia and Azerbaijan over Nagorno-Karabakh in 1992-1993. The Organization for Security and Cooperation in Europe's (OSCE) Minsk Group, which is chaired by France, the United States, and Russia and is spearheading the peace process, suggested in early 2001 that Tehran should be informed of progress. As a French diplomat explained:

> [Our aim is] to keep the Iranian authorities informed and to make it clear to them that no one will be kept aside. We certainly do not want to give the impression that we are acting against the interests of one or another country in the region. There cannot be a stable and long-lasting peace if it is not endorsed by all regional countries.[26]

A similarly inclusive approach in other regional fora, such as the Gulf Cooperation Council, would demonstrate an interest in and consideration towards Iranian concerns.

Visa Regulations and Travel Restrictions.

The treatment of Iranian visitors to the United States should be modified in some way. Greater concern about homeland security in the post-September 11, 2001, environment is normal and acceptable, but the Iranian regime plays up the difficulties Iranians encounter in getting visas and in actually trying to enter the United States.

A group of senior clerics associated with Ayatollah Mohammad Taqi Mesbah-Yazdi accepted an invitation to participate in a December 1999 conference at Georgetown University but withdrew when immigration officials at John F. Kennedy Airport in New York tried to fingerprint and photograph them. Iranian filmmaker Jafar Panahi, who was detained at John F. Kennedy Airport in April 2001 for not having a transit visa, complained publicly that he was mistreated and chained like a medieval prisoner. In February 2000 an Iranian wrestling team complained bitterly about the fingerprinting, and in May 2001 it boasted about the absence of fingerprinting.

A U.S. consular presence in Iran, which has not existed since 1979, would facilitate the visa application process and possibly reduce such events. The United States should continue to push for this, although it seems unlikely. In November 1999, Iranian Supreme Leader Ayatollah Seyyed Ali Husseini Khamenei explained that Tehran rejected such a proposal because "they [the Americans] want to open an intelligence-political site in Tehran to make contact with sold-out elements."[27] In January 2000 the director of the Kish Free Trade Zone said that a U.S. application to open a consulate there would be viewed favorably, but the Foreign Minister countered by saying, "we have a clear position towards the United States. We have no relations with the United States to talk about the opening of a U.S. consulate in any part of the country."[28]

World Trade Organization (WTO) Membership.

Iran first sought WTO membership in 1996, and in July 2001 the White House declared that its opposition to Iranian membership is "under review." WTO decisionmaking is based on consensus, and the United States has blocked Iran's application consistently (most recently in February 2002).[29] Other countries, such as France and the European Union, reportedly support Iranian membership, while the German Economics Minister pointed out that a normalization of ties with the United States would have to precede a successful membership application.[30]

There is domestic opposition to Iranian WTO membership, too. Unions have protested against membership on the grounds that it would lead to job losses.[31] Opposition also comes from leftists who favor a state-run economy, hardline isolationists, and conservative traditional merchants who want to maintain import controls because they have favorable licensing arrangements. A Ministry of Science, Research, and Technology official accused "unnamed parties" of blocking the country's WTO application.[32] The head of the Islamic Republic of Iran Customs Administration (IRICA) also has noted that certain organizations, which he refused to identify, oppose joining the WTO because removal of tariff barriers and subsidies would eliminate their advantage.[33]

Iranian officials normally blame the United States regarding the WTO issue. Washington would eliminate this grievance by allowing Iranian membership. Just as importantly the role of the state in the economy would be reduced and privatization would progress. Iranian economic interaction with the rest of the world would increase, and as Iranians recognize this interdependence they would have a greater interest in reducing actions that alienate the country from the international community.

POLICY CONSTRAINTS: THE WHITE HOUSE AND THE LAW

Any initiatives will require awareness of U.S. policy towards Iran, which was spelled out in several statements from the White House. President George W. Bush in a January 2002 statement specified a desired change in Iranian behavior.[34]

> Well, first of all, Iran must be a contributor in the war against terror; that our nation and our fight against terror will uphold the doctrine, either you're with us or against us; and any nation that thwarts our ability to rout terror out where it exists will be held to account, one way or the other.

As Iranian students held demonstration in July 2002, President Bush specified another aspect of U.S. policy on Iran.[35] "The people of Iran want the same freedoms, human rights, and opportunities as people around the world," he said. "Their government should listen to their hopes." The President added, "As Iran's people move towards a future defined by greater freedom, greater tolerance, they will have no better friend than the United States of America."

"The United States wants to see a democratic and prosperous Iran, integrated into the global economy," a top National Security Council (NSC) official said in an August 2002 speech.[36] He said that U.S. policy towards Iran follows two tracks, one of which publicly identifies the unacceptable aspects of Iranian behavior—"sponsorship of terror, pursuit of WMD, and repression of the clearly expressed desires of the Iranian people for freedom and democracy." The other track lays out a vision of partnership and support for the Iranian people.

U.S. policy is not about imposing change on Iran, but it will support Iranians' quest for self-determination, the NSC official said.[37] Nor is U.S. policy about factions or individuals in the Iranian governmental apparatus.

> U.S. policy is . . . about supporting those who want freedom, human rights, democracy, and economic and educational opportunity for themselves and their fellow countrymen and women.

In addition to White House policies, several laws and regulations impose restrictions and limits on possible initiatives regarding Iran. Only one of these laws, the Foreign Assistance Act of 1961 (Public Law 87-195), is relevant to the policy recommendations discussed above.[38] This act bans U.S. foreign assistance to governments supporting international terrorism, and the State Department has identified Iran as a state sponsor of terrorism since January 1984.[39]

Section 307 of the Foreign Assistance Act of 1961 states that Iran and other state sponsors of terrorism cannot benefit from U.S. contributions to international organizations. The United States would reduce its contribution to the international program in a proportionate share. This means that U.S. contributions to the UNODC are reduced in proportion to UNODC contributions to Iranian counternarcotics activities. U.S. contributions to UNICEF and the International Atomic Energy Agency (IAEA) are exempt from this restriction, and this provision does not apply to disaster relief aid. Section 620A permits the President to waive the restrictions if this is in the national interest.

MONITORING AND EVALUATION

The recommendations in the previous section could have an impact on Iran at the grass-roots level and especially among people who have had little prior interaction with Americans. The recommendations will not be very effective, however, if the Iranian public does not know that the United States is responsible. For example, the earthquake assistance that the United States provided in 2002 was delivered by chartered aircraft and by non-U.S. crews. And if Iran does gain WTO membership, Tehran will almost certainly claim that this is a diplomatic victory for it and another reflection of failed U.S. efforts to isolate it.

Getting this information to the Iranian public will not be easy due to serious media restrictions. The official Islamic Republic of Iran Broadcasting (IRIB) runs all the radio and television stations, and its hard-line bias often is criticized by Iranians themselves.

Foreign radio stations that broadcast in the Persian language are very popular in Iran, because they provide relatively unbiased news about international events, offer a platform for Iranians who do not have access to state media, and in one case, carry entertaining programs. Among these foreign stations are the British Broadcasting Corporation, Deutsche Welle, Radio France International, Kol Yisrael, Radio Beijing, NHK Radio Japan, Voice of America, and Voice of Russia.

The U.S.-sponsored Radio Farda began broadcasting to Iran in December 2002, having replaced the 4-year-old Persian Service of Radio Free Europe/Radio Liberty. Radio Farda is on the air 24 hours a day and is available via FM, shortwave, and satellite signal. Its target audience is the under-30 population, so it broadcasts pop music to attract these listeners. It also has 15-minute newscasts at the top of the hour 20 times a day and 3-minute newscasts at the half-hour 20 times a day. Four times a day it transmits 30-minute newsmagazines.

Satellite television is popular. The impact of Los Angeles-based stations that are run by Iranian expatriates, such as Pars TV and

NITV, was demonstrated in the week starting October 21, 2001, when NITV urged Iranians to take to the streets to protest against the government. Iranians actually did so, rioting after losing a World Cup soccer qualifying match. They chanted slogans against the government and destroyed property. During several days of demonstrations in Tehran in June 2003, satellite broadcasts again urged Iranians to take to the streets and to confront the regime's security forces.

Not only is satellite television popular, it is illegal.[40] There are periodic police sweeps in which satellite dishes are confiscated, and at the end of April 2003 President Hojatoleslam Seyyed Mohammad Khatami-Ardakani and Speaker of Parliament Hojatoleslam Mehdi Karrubi complained about unauthorized jamming of satellite television signals.[41] Reporters Without Borders noted the jamming of foreign television and radio signals in June 2003.[42] As satellite receiving equipment becomes smaller and less expensive, it will become more readily available to the Iranian public, thereby making it easier to communicate directly with the Iranian people.

The Iranian print media also operates under numerous restrictions, the most onerous being the undefined "red-lines," the crossing of which often leads to a publication's closure.[43] The courts have closed approximately 80 publications since April 2000, and Reporters Without Borders refers to Iran as "the biggest jail for journalists in the Middle East" in its annual report for 2002.[44]

One of the means by which Iranians are overcoming the state's attempt to monopolize information sources is by turning to the Internet. Persian language websites (for example, *www.rooznegar.com*, *www.emrooz.org*, *www.alliran.net*), as well as foreign news sources, are increasingly popular with Iranians. Iranians also exchange information in chat rooms and blogs. The Minister of Post, Telegraph, and Telephone estimated that 15 million Iranians would have access to the Internet by March 2005.[45] The Internet, therefore, is another way to publicize U.S. initiatives.

Constant monitoring of Iranian media, interviews with Iranians living in the United States, and traveler surveys would provide the necessary input on the effectiveness of the recommended initiatives. This, in turn, would facilitate making adjustments to those initiatives that are having the desired effect, elimination of the ineffective ones, and adoption of new ones.

CONCLUSION

The United States cannot ignore Iran and hope that Tehran's attitudes will soften and its behavior change with time, because of the threat it will pose in the near future. Iran is pursuing programs to produce nuclear, biological, and chemical weapons, regardless of its status in the Treaty on the Nonproliferation of Nuclear Weapons (NPT), the Biological Weapons Convention (BWC), and the Chemical Weapons Convention (CWC).[46] Most Intelligence Community agencies believe that the United States will face an ICBM threat from Iran by 2015, and Iran's missile inventory already is among the largest in the Middle East.[47] Iran remained "the most active state sponsor of terrorism during 2002," according to the U.S. State Department's annual *Patterns of Global Terrorism—2002* report, providing support for violent groups such as Lebanese Hizballah, Hamas, and the Palestine Islamic Jihad (PIJ).

The policy recommendations described above are unlikely to affect Iranian strategic thinking or its international behavior in the short-term. But these steps will resonate with young Iranians who were born after the revolution and who have become disenchanted and frustrated with their country's rulers. These individuals hope for a better future, and a hearts and minds campaign will persuade them that the United States is a friend that wants to help them achieve that future. Such a campaign is, furthermore, in line with the Bush administration's policy of supporting the Iranian people.

ENDNOTES - CHAPTER 5

1. According to the UN Population Division, the population in 2000 was 66.43 million; *http://esa.un.org/unpp/p2k0data.asp*. The Central Intelligence Agency's World Factbook estimates that as of July 2002, the population was 66,622,704.

2. Mark J. Roberts, "Iran and the 'Great Satan,'" *Joint Forces Quarterly*, Autumn 1995.

3. William Beeman, "Images of the Great Satan: Representations of the United States in the Iranian Revolution," in Nikkie R. Keddie, ed., *Religion and Politics in*

Iran-Shi'ism from Quietism to Revolution, New Haven: Yale University Press, 1983, pp. 191, 192.

4. *Ibid.*, p. 216.

5. *Ibid.*, p. 201.

6. Elaine Sciolino, *Persian Mirrors–The Elusive Face of Iran*, New York: The Free Press, 2000, pp. 28, 43-45.

7. *Ibid.*, pp. 29, 34.

8. Afshin Molavi, *Persian Pilgrimages—Journeys Across Iran*, New York: W. W. Norton & Co., 2002, pp. 79-82.

9. *Ibid.*, pp. 102-104.

10. *Ibid.*, p. 142.

11. Robin Wright, *The Last Great Revolution*, New York: Alfred A. Knopf, 2000, p. xv.

12. *Ibid.*, p. 194.

13. *Ibid.*, pp. 252-253.

14. Nazgol Ashouri, "Polling in Iran: Surprising Questions," *Policywatch #757*, The Washington Institute of Near East Policy, May 14, 2003.

15. Islamic Republic News Agency (IRNA), September 22, 2002. Iran's press corps accused Ayandeh Research Institute of taking money from the Washington-based Gallup Organization to fabricate the poll. Richard Burkholder, director of international polling at Gallup, told RFE/RL's Persian Service that Gallup is a private company and is not connected with the U.S. Government; and when Gallup pays foreign companies to conduct polls, they use questions and methodology developed by Gallup. National Institute for Research and Opinion Polls director Behruz Geranpayeh said that the Iranian legislature's research center commissioned the survey; IRNA, December 31, 2002.

16. Iranian Students News Agency (ISNA), March 23, 2003.

17. The Iranian Students Opinion Polls Center conducted the survey; IRNA, April 14, 2003.

18. Public prosecutor's office representative Ali Asqar Tashakori discussing

Vahid Sinai and Mehdi Abbasirad, cited by IRNA, December 31, 2003.

19. Jahangir Amuzegar, "Iran's Crumbling Revolution," *Foreign Affairs*, January/February 2003.

20. USAID Press Release, March 10, 1997.

21. *Ibid.*, July 3, 2002, U.S. State Department's Office of International Information Programs, *usinfo.state.gov*.

22. See A. William Samii, "Drug Abuse: Iran's 'Thorniest Problem,'" *Brown Journal of World Affairs*, Winter/Spring 2003.

23. Health Ministry public relations department chief Hushmand Sefidi, cited by IRNA, May 22, 2003; Health Ministry official Mohammad Mehdi Guya, cited by IRNA, May 20, 2003.

24. Prisons Organization chief Morteza Bakhtiari, cited by IRNA, January 16, 2003.

25. National Security Council official Zalmay Khalilzad and U.S. Deputy Assistant Secretary of State Ryan Crocker reportedly met with Iran's representative to the United Nations, Mohammad Javad Zarif, and/or other senior Iranian officials and Islamic Revolution Guards Corps officers in January and March; UPI, March 26, 2003, and *The Washington Post*, April 18, 2003. Tehran denied that any discussions occurred, with Foreign Minister Kamal Kharrazi saying that Iran is not ready for the restoration of diplomatic relations with the United States, "because the United States is not ready for the kind of relations based on mutual respect among countries;" AP, April 21, 2003.

26. Former French Ambassador to Tehran and Minsk Group co-Chairman Philippe de Suremain, in an interview with Jean-Christophe Peuch, "Iran Offers To Mediate In Nagorno-Karabakh Dispute," RFE/RL Weekday Magazine, July 25, 2001.

27. Ayatollah Ali Khamenei's speech to students and staff of Sharif University in Tehran, Voice of the Islamic Republic of Iran, November 22, 1999.

28. Foreign Minister Kamal Kharrazi, cited by IRNA, January 24, 2000.

29. Frances Williams, "Iran's bid to join WTO is blocked by U.S.," *Financial Times*, February 14, 2002.

30. IRNA, April 9, 2003, April 17, 2003. German Economics Minister Werner Mueller, cited by IRNA, August 15, 2002.

31. IRNA, November 9, 2001.

32. Mohammad Nahavandian, cited by IRNA, October 22, 2002.

33. IRICA President Masud Karbasian, interview with *Hamshahri,* October 20, 2002.

34. Remarks by the President in a meeting with his economic team, The Oval Office, January 10, 2002, U.S. Department of State's Office of International Information Programs, *usinfo.state.gov.*

35. Statement by the President, July 12, 2002, U.S. State Department's Office of International Information Programs, *usinfo.state.gov.*

36. Special assistant to the president and senior director for Southwest Asia, Near East and North Africa on the National Security Council Zalmay Khalilzad's speech at the Washington Institute of Near East Policy, August 2, 2002, U.S. State Department's Office of International Information Programs, *usinfo.state.gov.*

37. *Ibid.*

38. Kenneth Katzman, *U.S.-Iran Relations: An Analytic Compendium of U.S. Policies, Laws, and Regulations,* The Atlantic Council of the United States Occasional Paper, December 1990, pp. 59-63.

39. State sponsorship means that Iran provides terrorists with safe-haven, travel documents, arms, training, and technical expertise, state support, or toleration.

40. A good study on this issue is Steven Barraclough, "Satellite Television in Iran: Prohibition, Imitation, and Reform," *Middle Eastern Studies,* Vol. 37, n. 3, July 2001.

41. IRNA, April 22, 2003.

42. *http://www.rsf.org/article.php3?id_article=7151.*

43. See A. William Samii, "The Contemporary Iranian News Media, 1998-1999," *Middle East Review of International Affairs (MERIA) Journal,* Vol. 3, n. 4, December 1999; and A. William Samii, "Sisyphus' Newsstand: The Iranian Press Under Khatami," *MERIA Journal,* Vol. 5 n. 3, September 2001.

44. *http://www.rsf.org/article.php3?id_article=1438*

45. Minister of Post, Telegraph, and Telephone Ahmad Motamedi, cited by *Iran Daily*, March 10, 2003.

46. Central Intelligence Agency, "Unclassified Report to Congress on the Acquisition of Technology Relating to Weapons of Mass Destruction and Advanced Conventional Munitions, 1 January Through 30 June 2002," http://www.cia.gov/cia/publications/bian/bian_apr_2003.htm.

47. National Intelligence Council, "Foreign Missile Developments and the Ballistic Missile Threat Through 2015," *Unclassified Summary of a National Intelligence Estimate*, December 2001, *http://www.cia.gov/nic/pubs/other_products/Unclassifiedballisticmissilefinal.htm*.

CHAPTER 6

U.S.-IRANIAN STRATEGIC COOPERATION SINCE 1979

Geoffrey Kemp

U.S. attempts at strategic cooperation with Iran have evolved through a number of stages since the traumatic revolution of 1979. The first phase lasted through the 1980s and ended with the death of Khomeini in 1989. The second phase witnessed the Gulf War and the efforts by President Rafsanjani and, later, President Clinton to establish some sort of *modus vivendi*. However it was accompanied by harsher U.S. sanctions and strident anti-Israeli behavior and rhetoric from Iran. The third phase began with the surprise election of Mohammad Khatami in 1997 and the new hopes for U.S.-Iranian rapprochement. It ended with the fall of Saddam Hussein. The current phase of the relationship will be dominated by postwar Iraq, Iran's continued support for terrorism and the advanced status of Iran's nuclear program. One way or another a climax to U.S.-Iranian relations is likely in the coming year or so.

Phase 1: 1979-89.

The first years of the revolution were dominated by the 14-month hostage crisis--November 1979-January 1981--precipitated when Iran, in violation of international law, took American diplomats into its custody in Tehran. Dramas of the hostage crisis had a profound and dramatic impact on American public opinion and politics. It was one of the key reasons President Carter lost the 1980 election to Ronald Reagan. Two months earlier, Iran was invaded by Iraq and the 8-year Iran-Iraq War began. Despite Saddam's aggression, the United States was quietly pleased to see the regime facing a new major threat and while the United States professed neutrality, there were expectations and hopes that Saddam's forces would topple the Ayatollah's new government.

Thus when the Reagan administration assumed office in January 1981, it had no interest in modifying the tough line policy towards the Iranian regime, but as the war bogged down in Iran, the issue was not on the front burner of the new administration.

It assumed much more importance in June 1982 when, against expectations, the Iranian army successfully expelled Iraq from Iran and then made the fateful decision to carry the war onto the Arabian Peninsula, thereby threatening not only Iraq but also the oil-rich Arab monarchies. This coincided with a period in Iran when revolutionary zeal was at its peak and the hope of spreading Islamic revolutions all around the region was openly talked about. The problem was that the regime's zealotry was not shared by most of its neighbors, and Iran found itself isolated with the exception of support from Syria and Shiite factions in Lebanon. The United States concluded that a successful Iranian offensive against Iraq would pose a major strategic threat to the region and therefore a distinct "tilt" towards Iraq began. In other words, the first truly strategic decision the United States made after the hostage crisis was to oppose Iran in a forceful and effective way. Iran became subjected to a widespread, worldwide embargo orchestrated by the United States called Operation STAUNCH, while Iraq, on the other hand, was openly supported by the majority of Arab states, Europe, the Soviet Union and, more circumspectly, the United States.

At the beginning of the second Reagan administration, it was clear that there would be no early end to the Iran-Iraq War. Iran's lack of spare parts for its sophisticated U.S.-made Air Force was a major constraint on its military operations, and the regime was losing vast numbers of soldiers in suicide missions trying to breakthrough the Shatt al-Arab barrier and take the city of Basra. It was the extraordinary constraints on Iran's Air Force and missile capabilities that persuaded the Iranians to do the unthinkable--consider doing business with the United States and Israel--by now known as the Great Satan and Little Satan, respectively.

This was the beginning of the ill-fated Iran-Contra scandal involving a deal to trade arms for American hostages held in Lebanon by pro-Iranian groups, with the residuary benefit that some of the money from the arms sales would go to the Nicaraguan contras. The rationale for the willingness of the White House to consider this overture to Iran, was based on a highly controversial intelligence analysis that believed that there were moderate forces in revolutionary Iran who were prepared to compromise and reach a rapprochement with the United States. It was argued that this would be in American interests because of parallel concerns about growing Soviet influence in Iran and the fear that Iran would ultimately fall under Soviet hands, which would have significantly raised the strategic risks to the United States in the Persian Gulf region. At that time the Soviet offensive in Afghanistan was still in high gear.

While such an approach to Iran was bitterly contested by both the Pentagon and the State Department, the arms-for-hostage deal nevertheless proceeded and very nearly destroyed the second Reagan administration. However, very few arms found their way to Iran, but the United States increased its support for Iraq, especially real time intelligence sharing. U.S. attitudes toward Iran became increasingly feisty, and towards the end of the war the United States became directly involved in the fighting as part of a multilateral operation to protect Arab oil tankers that were being attacked by the Iranians. On July 3, 1988, the U.S. warship *Vincennes* accidentally shot down an Iranian airliner, killing 290 civilians. The end of the war came soon after this event. Iran was a defeated power which had been humiliated and isolated by the international community and subject to the most brutal attacks by Saddam Hussein's forces which were using chemical weapons. At no time did the international community protest beyond nominal utterances, and to this day Iran's sufferings and humiliation during this period are felt by all Iranians, whether moderate, hard-liner, or anything else.

Phase 2: 1989-96.

The end of the Iran-Iraq War was followed a year later by the death of the Ayatollah Khomeini. This opened the possibility of a thaw in U.S.-Iranian relations. In his inaugural address on January 20, 1989, President George H. Bush appeared to reach out to Iran when, in reference to the American hostages still held in Lebanon by pro-Iranian groups, he said, "today there are Americans who are held against their will in foreign lands, there are Americans who are unaccounted for. Assistance can be shown here and will be long remembered. Good will begets good will."

The Iranians read this as a signal that if they cooperated in getting the release of the hostages, they would be rewarded in some way. Most of the hostages were released. However, no rewards were forthcoming. Iran remained a highly sensitive political issue for the White House. George Bush, himself, had been tainted by the Iran-Contra scandal and had no desire to follow in the steps of Carter and Reagan and burn his fingers on overtures to this prickly regime.

Another opportunity for cooperation came during the 1990-91 Gulf War. Iran made a strategic decision to sit out the war and mount no serious opposition to the American-led coalition. Iran provided refuge for fleeing Iraqi airplanes and never turned them over to the Saddam Hussein regime during or after the Gulf War. From the Iranian point of view, they had made a strategic decision to help the coalition by not interfering. They expected at the end of war that there might be some gesture from the administration.

In a postwar speech, Bush offered four key challenges for the new Middle East: to create shared security arrangements, to control weapons of mass destruction, to promote a comprehensive Arab-Israeli peace and to promote economic development. These goals became part of the cornerstone of the Madrid Peace Conference which was convened in November 1991. Iran was not invited, not consulted, and left out of the negotiations. It responded by hosting a gathering of radical states opposed to the Madrid Conference. The messages coming from Iran during this period remained mixed. The new President Ali Akbar Hashemi Rafsanjani was considered more pragmatic than Ayatollah Khomeini. However, it was not until the Clinton administration came into office in 1992 that the Rafsanjani government attempted any new initiatives, and this was not until several years into the administration.

The Clinton administration came into office in January 1993, and as is always the case, a reappraisal of U.S. policy in the Persian Gulf was undertaken. The administration criticized the Reagan-Bush legacy arguing that the efforts prior to August 1990 to balance Iraq against Iran and tilt towards Iraq during the Iran-Iraq War were based on faulty thinking. The Clinton team did not believe that a regional balance of power was sustainable. The United States needed to treat both Iran and Iraq as "backlash or rogue" states that should be contained and isolated.

Clinton administration policy toward Iran can be broken down into three periods. The first period, May 1993 to May 1995, saw the enunciation of the "dual containment" strategy as an effort to keep both Iran and Iraq impotent: the United States would become the guarantor of Gulf security, act as the "balancer" in the region, and deploy sufficient military power to deter, or if necessary defeat, both Iraq and Iran in a future confrontation.

However, it was clear from the beginning that a differentiated policy of containment toward the two countries would be pursued. Iraq was subject to UN-mandated international sanctions resulting from the invasion and occupation of Kuwait in August 1990. U.S. policy was to eventually remove the Saddam Hussein regime. In the case of Iran, U.S. policy was initially more benign, the focus being to change key elements of Iranian policy, namely support for international terrorism, rejection of the Arab-Israeli peace process (including Israel's right to exist), development of weapons of mass destruction, and violations of human rights and international law. These objectives have remained consistent since 1993.

Meanwhile, Iranian President Rafsanjani sought to open Iran to the outside world and to attract the foreign capital Iran needed to rebuild after nearly a decade of war and revolution. A key part of Rafsanjani's new policy of openness was easing Iran's tense relationship with the United States. He believed that a more open policy with Washington would facilitate Iran's economic development, particularly in the energy sector. Much of the National Iranian Oil Company's drilling equipment had been purchased in the late 1970s and was badly in need of modernization.

Iran pursued Rafsanjani's "moderate" foreign policy and sought to reform the economy. Parts of the Iranian economy were liberalized and opened to outside competition. In numerous interviews with western media, Rafsanjani sought to downplay the years of enmity with the United States and emphasized Iran's newfound openness to change. Iran also worked to improve relations with American's closest allies, especially Saudi Arabia and the European Union (EU).

The United States pursued an ambiguous policy concerning economic relations with Iran. While the official policy called for "dual containment," the reality was that the United States continued to trade with Iran, and U.S. oil companies continued to purchase Iranian oil and sell it on the world market. Then, in 1995, came a U.S. decision to impose unilateral sanctions on Iran and forbid U.S. companies from doing business in the Islamic Republic. This was a result of two converging pressures. First, the administration's efforts to convince Europeans and Japan that U.S. economic isolation or containment of Iran was a good idea was offset by the reality that the United States was Iran's premier trading partner. Second, by 1995 anti-Iranian voices in the U.S. Congress had convinced the administration that further economic sanctions on Iran would be imposed the Congress. So the executive branch itself issued an executive order banning further trade in May 1995.

Ironically, the catalyst of this decision was Iran's surprise announcement of an offer to an American company, Conoco, to develop an Iranian off-shore gas field in the Persian Gulf at South Pars. Conoco officials had worked for many years on the project and beat out the French company, Total, for the contract. The announcement sent shockwaves through Washington. Although the agreement clearly violated the spirit of dual containment, senior State Department officials were forced to admit that the deal was legal. For their part, senior Iranian officials, such as President Rafsanjani, may have hoped that the Conoco deal would help to open a new period of U.S.-Iranian relations and to justify Tehran's foreign policy and economic reforms. Thus began a second, more confrontational period of the Clinton administration's policy toward Iran which remained in place until May 1997.

During this second phase, the debate in Washington was between hawks and superhawks. Few, if any, decisionmakers were in favor of offering Iran an "olive branch." The hawks were those who wished to further isolate Iran economically, while trying to find ways to cooperate with Europe in order to increase pressure on the Iranian government to change its policies. The superhawks were those who saw no possibility of negotiating with or moderating the actions of the Iranian regime--what was necessary was a change of regime.

Phase 3: The Khatami Years.

The surprise election of Mohammad Khatami in May 1997 dramatically changed American attitudes towards Iran and ushered in the third period of Clinton's Iran policy. The election threw the Clinton administration into something of a furor. Khatami's overtures to the United States following his election included a remarkable interview with CNN Correspondent Christianne Amanpour on January 7, 1998, where he called for a "dialogue of civilizations" between the United States and Iran. Over the coming months there was a flurry of activity suggesting that a breakthrough in relations might be possible. In June 1998, Madeline Albright made a speech at the Asia Society calling for a road map to better relations, and President Clinton issued a statement at the time of the World Cup soccer match between the United States and Iran, "as we cheer today's game between American and Iranian athletes, I hope it can be another step towards ending the strains between our nations."

The United States then made another strategic gesture to Iran on October 8, 1999, by placing the premier opposition group to the Iranian regime, the Mujahideen e-Khalq, on the terrorist list making them susceptible to laws that freeze their financial assets in the United States, deny U.S. visas to their families, and subject Americans who assist them financially or with weaponry to 10 years in prison. This gesture to the new Iranian leadership was reportedly due in part to President Khatami's decision to replace the former intelligence Minister, Ali Fallahian, an architect of the terror campaigns, as well as other controversial personnel in the old Iranian cabinet.

The Iranian direct response to these gestures was tepid and did little to mollify the critics of Clinton who believed that he was reaching out too far. The unresolved issue of the June 1996 Khobar Towers terrorist bombing outside Dhahran still haunted U.S. officials, as did the continued Iranian stridency towards Israel. Nevertheless, the first four years of Khatami's presidency were ones of high hopes for better U.S.-Iranian relations. A lot of track two activity occurred but no clear breakthroughs. During this period Iranians remained bitterly divided on the wisdom of strategic cooperation with the

United States and displayed very ambivalent behavior.

Khatami's reelection in 2001 held out hopes that perhaps the process could be restarted with the election of George W. Bush and his Vice President, Dick Cheney. Cheney, as Chief Executive Officer of Halliburton prior to joining the administration, had given several speeches questioning the wisdom of continued sanctions against Iran. The real opportunity came after September 11, 2001, and the inevitability of a U.S. war in Afghanistan which would deeply affect Iran. Iran feared the Taliban and quietly was delighted at their overthrow. During that war, the Iranians did cooperate with the United States and were helpful in efforts to form the interim Afghan government at meetings in Bonn in December of that year. Again, it was clear that those elements in the Iranian government interested in better relations were using the Afghan war as an opportunity to reach out. However, at the same time, more revolutionary elements were increasing their strategic cooperation with terrorist groups in the Middle East, notably Hezbollah, Hamas, Palestinian Islamic Jihad, and, ultimately, the Palestinian Authority. The discovery of the Iranian arms heading for Palestine on the Karine-A merchant ship, poisoned all hopes for rapprochement in the early days of the Bush administration. In fact, it was following this incident that Iran was placed on the "axis of evil" and clearly put in the sights of America's new policy on preemption. Iranian meddling in Afghanistan after the war did not help their case either.

As it became clear in the summer and fall of 2002 that a crisis with Iraq, in one form or another, was inevitable, U.S. officials met secretly with Iranian counterparts to assure that, if there was a war with Iraq, Iran would play the same role it did during the first Gulf War. From what is known of the record, Iran's behavior during the Iraq War was relatively cooperative, but in the aftermath of the war it is clear that the charges of Iranian intervention have to be taken seriously. Again this reflects a bitter debate in Iran about the wisdom of strategic rapprochement with the United States at this time. Reformers, by and large, see the fall of Saddam Hussein as an opportunity to open up to the administration, accept the reality of American power in the region, and move on to resolve the horrendous domestic problems they face. Alternatively, the hard-liners see the American threat as more ominous than ever. Iranian strategic planners were not unhappy with the situation in Iraq prior to Saddam's fall. He was, after all, contained by the United States and was placed under a strict international arms embargo. Iranians now worry that a new, strong Iraq will emerge which will clearly pose threats to them.

Phase 4: Future Prospects for Cooperation.

The coming months will be some of the most critical in U.S.-Iranian relations. The dramatic news that became public in the latter months of 2002 and confirmed in February 2003, that Iran's nuclear infrastructure was far more advanced than the public had been led to believe, puts the possibility of the Iranian bomb front and center and poses a most severe challenge to America. This, paralleled with the uncertainty in Iraq, means that sooner or later some confrontation with Iran over nuclear weapons, terrorism, and involvement in Iraq is inevitable unless the Iranians choose this moment to walk away from the Arab-Israeli conflict, reign in their terrorism, and find some way to finesse their nuclear program within the confines of the Nuclear Non-Proliferation Treaty (NPT).

If Iran decides that the time has come for a political dialogue with Washington, the most difficult task will be to persuade its leaders that its security will be enhanced if it abandons terrorism and defers a nuclear weapons program.

However, Iran will argue that it still lives in a nuclear neighborhood. Israel, Pakistan, and India will be presented as evidence of the nuclear asymmetries. So long as a dialogue focuses on these regional discrepancies, little progress is likely. Israel will not contemplate negotiating about its bomb until a generation of peace between itself and its neighbors has passed. Likewise, Pakistan will not forsake the bomb so long as India is perceived as a threat. India, always concerned about China, will not abandon its bomb until the United States, Russia, China, the U.K., and France do likewise. Thus, it is quite unrealistic for Iran to expect a nuclear quid pro quo for its own restraint. This is where carrots, as well as sticks, become important. If Iran ends military and financial support to terrorist groups, signs the additional protocol of the NPT, and complies with the statutes of the Chemical Weapons Convention, real progress may be possible. The carrots could be considerable. The United States could help resolve bilateral issues, including the return of financial assets held since the revolution and the end of executive and legislative trade sanctions. Under these circumstances the United States should be prepared to work with Iran in developing investment opportunities in the region, including energy projects.

If there is future regional cooperation, Iraq and Iran must participate. However, much will depend on the configuration and policies of a new Iraqi regime and how much residual control will rest with the United States or UN occupation forces. Iran's leaders will be very suspicious of the United States and its role in postwar Iraq, especially given the presence of a formidable U.S. military force. To convince them that the United States seeks cooperative security arrangements rather than coercive dominance will not be easy, especially since the two key U.S. demands of Iran--abandon terrorism and stop the nuclear weapons program--are linked in Iranian eyes to their national security.

Iran faces tough political choices with regard to its U.S. policy, but the Bush administration also needs to address Iran's security needs if terror is stopped and the bomb put on hold. It is unrealistic to expect Iran to stop its missile program or slowdown the modernization of its conventional forces absent a new cooperative regional security environment. For it is not only weapons of mass destruction that determine security priorities. The future of the U.S. military presence in the Arab world and the size and configuration of Iraq's restructured armed forces will be key factors influencing Iranian perceptions.

The coming months will be critical for U.S.-Iranian relations. The dramatic news that became public in the latter months of 2002 and was confirmed in February 2003, that Iran's nuclear infrastructure was far more advanced than the public had been led to believe, puts the possibility of the Iranian bomb front and center and poses a most severe challenge to the United States and to Middle East regional security and the global non-proliferation regime. This development, paralleled by the uncertainty over developments in Iraq, means that, sooner or later, some confrontation with Iran over nuclear weapons, terrorism, and involvement in Iraq is inevitable unless the Iranians choose to moderate their policy towards the Arab-Israeli conflict, reign in their support for terrorism, and find some way to finesse their nuclear program within the confines of the NPT.

The advanced status of the Iranian nuclear program has been revealed most explicitly in recent visits to the country by IAEA inspectors. It will soon be known whether or not Iran will comply with international pressures to sign the Additional Protocol to provide more transparency about its nuclear activities. Even if Iran takes this step, there will be many skeptics who will argue that such action will merely delay the day when Iran can get the bomb. The good news is that the international community, particularly the Europeans, Russians, and Japanese, now seem to share American concerns about what the Iranians are up to.

By early 2003, the Russians and the Europeans were becoming as worried as the Americans about the Iranian nuclear program and, while the war in Iraq set cooperation back a pace, there is no doubt that the initiatives undertaken by the United States in probing the IAEA to be more assertive towards Iran has been reciprocated in Moscow and Brussels. This is a very positive development in view of the laidback European attitudes of the past and the formerly uncooperative behavior of Russia. It does suggest that by consistently dwelling on the problems posed by an Iranian bomb, the U.S. Government and U.S. nongovernmental organizations (NGOs) have had an influence on the thinking of key partners. Whether or not this combination of pressure will affect the regime's behavior is but one element in the debate about how to handle this dangerous and difficult problem. The other hope is that the Iranians themselves, as a result of rational and careful debate, will come to see that nuclear weapons do not serve their national interest even though they have incentives, and to some extent, the right to develop a self-sufficient nuclear energy program.

Thus, there may be a small window of time during which Iranian opinion can be influenced towards restraint. This outcome is by no means certain and will depend upon many contingencies, but it is surely worth making a determined effort to have constructive input into the Iranian debate. It is interesting to note that on another issue of importance to Iran, namely its policy towards Israel, the Iranian Parliament has become more open to questioning the dogma of the regime which has been to deny Israel's right to exist and support groups that advocate the use of force against Israel. Now a number of senior Iranians, including members of Parliament, are asking the very fundamental question: how does a policy of confrontation with Israel serve Iranian national interests? Since this is one of the key issues that bedevil U.S.-Iranian relations, it is a fair question. The objective, therefore, of stimulating any debate in Iran about nuclear weapons must be to have Iranians ask the same question: How would the bomb serve our national interests?

If Iran continues to refuse to have a formal official dialogue with the United States to discuss each country's concerns, the probabilities for dangerous encounters will increase. Iran will not *kowtow* publicly to American demands, especially in view of the difficulties the United States continues to face in postwar Iraq. However if approached with a serious set of proposals, Iran's leaders might rethink their agenda. The United States should explore the possibilities for better relations while continuing its message on terrorism and WMD. If this opportunity is missed, the likelihood of confrontation will increase and, at an indeterminate time, an Iranian bomb will materialize.

CHAPTER 7

THE CHALLENGES OF U.S. PREVENTIVE MILITARY ACTION

Michael Eisenstadt

For some U.S. policymakers and military planners, Israel's 1981 raid on Iraq's Osiraq nuclear reactor may serve as an object lesson regarding the potential benefits of preventive military action against Iran's nuclear program. Not widely appreciated is how risky and difficult the Osiraq raid was, and how the factors which ensured its success make attempting similar action against Iran's nuclear facilities so challenging. U.S. preventive action against Iran's nuclear program would necessarily bear little resemblance to the Osiraq raid, and the results would unlikely be as decisive and lasting.

The success of the Osiraq operation obscured difficulties in planning and execution. The raid was the longest mission the Israeli Air Force had undertaken at that time. The strike package (eight F-16s escorted by six F-15s) flew nearly the entire 2,000 km mission over hostile airspace, yet managed to achieve surprise. The F-16s were operating very close to their maximum unrefueled combat radius; had they been challenged by Jordanian, Saudi, or Iraqi aircraft, they would have lacked endurance to engage in evasive maneuver or sustained aerial combat. The raid on Osiraq pushed Israel's air force to the very limits of its operational capabilities.[1]

Several factors contributed to the Israeli success in 1981:

- The Osiraq reactor—a highly visible and vulnerable target—was the centerpiece of Iraq's nuclear program, and its destruction set the effort several years back.[2] Learning from this experience, Iraq subsequently dispersed and hid its nuclear infrastructure. Other proliferators—including Iran—have since done the same.[3]

- Israel may have benefited from French aid in destroying Osiraq. French intelligence reportedly emplaced a homing beacon at Osiraq to help Israeli pilots locate the facility or target a critical underground structure there.[4]

- For Israel, Iraq was an enemy state that was pledged to its destruction. For Israeli cabinet members who voted in favor of the raid, the imperative to eliminate a perceived existential threat ultimately overshadowed countervailing political considerations.

- Iraq was at war with Iran at the time, and was thus constrained in its ability to strike back against Israel. Retaliation eventually took the form of an unsuccessful Iraqi attempt to strike the Israeli nuclear reactor at Dimona with missiles during the 1991 Gulf War.

Many of the conditions that were conducive to success at Osiraq, however, do not apply to the case of U.S. preventive action against Iran's nuclear program. In particular:

- Key elements of Iran's nuclear program are dispersed and concealed. Accordingly, it would not be possible to disable Iran's nuclear program by a single strike against a solitary facility; multiple simultaneous strikes against several sites would probably be required.

- While foreign technicians and advisors have access to parts of the declared civilian nuclear program (notably the Bushehr power plant), facilities involved in any clandestine parallel program are almost certainly off-limits to foreigners.

- Though relations between Washington and Tehran are tense and occasionally hostile, the United States is interested in encouraging political change in Iran, and in improving relations with that country. Preventive action might complicate, if not undermine, these efforts.

- Iran could respond to a preventive strike by retaliating against U.S. interests in Iraq, the Persian Gulf region, or against the United States itself, by means of Iranian agents or associated terrorist groups such as the Lebanese Hizballah.

For these reasons, preventive action against Iran (whether covert action involving U.S. intelligence assets or overt military action by U.S. military forces) is a much more complicated proposition than the Israeli strike on Osiraq. Significant intelligence and targeting challenges would have to be overcome, the potential for a nationalistic backlash in Iran and renewed tensions with U.S. allies would have to be managed, and Iranian retaliation would have to be deterred or disrupted.

Nonetheless, prevention must be given serious consideration for a number of reason: it is unclear whether the diplomatic option that the United States is now pursuing will bear fruit; solutions may be found to the intelligence, targeting, political, and security challenges of preventive action against Iran; and by keeping this option on the table, the United States can use the threat of prevention as a spur to multilateral diplomacy.

This chapter will thus assess the risks, challenges, and implications of prevention, assuming that the potential consequences of a nuclear Iran are sufficiently grave to justify consideration of such a potentially perilous course of action. It will not, however, evaluate the risks of *not* taking preventive action or the implications of a nuclear Iran for U.S. interests, which is a necessary element of any net assessment of the pros and cons of preventive action, but beyond the scope of this chapter.[5]

IRAN'S NUCLEAR PROGRAM: A HARD TARGET

Bushehr: Part of the Nuclear Target Set.

Iran's nuclear program has made steady progress. The power plant at Bushehr is finally approaching completion. According to Russian officials, Unit I at Bushehr may be completed by late 2003 or early 2004, with the first consignment of reactor fuel to be delivered during this timeframe.[6] Problems have dogged Iran's nuclear program from its inception. Russia originally undertook to complete Unit I by 1999, though technical and financial problems caused repeated delays. It is conceivable that new technical snafus, a Russian decision to hold-up the shipment of reactor components or fuel, or teething problems during reactor startup, could further delay completion of the project. Iranian officials have indicated, however, that the successful completion of Unit I might lead to contracts for additional nuclear power plants at Bushehr and Ahvaz, providing a powerful incentive for continued Russian cooperation.

Bushehr provides Iran with two potential routes to "the Bomb": low-enriched uranium fuel earmarked for Bushehr could be diverted and further enriched to weapons-grade material, or the reactor could be used to produce plutonium for weapons use.

Though not ideally suited for the purpose, Bushehr could produce enough plutonium for dozens of nuclear weapons per year. If Tehran were willing to violate its Nuclear Nonproliferation Treaty (NPT) commitments or withdraw from the NPT, Iran could separate truly prodigious quantities (scores of bombs worth) of weapons- or reactor-grade plutonium annually—depending on fuel burn-up. Although reactor-grade plutonium is not ideal for bombmaking (Heat and radioactivity makes it difficult and dangerous to work with, while its isotopic composition makes for an inefficient and unreliable bomb in rather crude weapons designs.), the United States demonstrated the military utility of reactor-grade plutonium in a 1962 underground nuclear explosive test.[7] Assuming that the Bushehr reactor comes on line in early 2004, Iran could start producing spent fuel containing plutonium by some time in 2005. Separation of plutonium from spent fuel and weaponization could take several months more, provided that Iran had the requisite know-how. Thus, Iran could conceivably produce a bomb using plutonium from Bushehr within three or four years.

Clandestine Fissile Material Production: Dispersed, Hardened, Hidden?

In response to detailed allegations by an expatriate Iranian opposition group, Iran has acknowledged that it is building a heavy-

116

water production plant and plans to build a 40MWt natural uranium research reactor at Arak, and that it is constructing a gas-centrifuge plant at Natanz. The existence of these facilities, confirmed by the International Atomic Energy Agency (IAEA) in a June 2003 report to its Board of Governors,[8] and Iran's prior failure to declare their existence, raises the troubling question of whether these facilities were formerly intended to be core elements of a clandestine weapons program.

Little is known about the natural uranium reactor that Iran plans to build at Arak, but Iranian officials have indicated that it will be a CANDU-type design intended for research purposes.[9] A typical 40MWt research reactor could produce sufficient plutonium for a few weapons a year. Construction of such a reactor usually takes 5-7 years, so it will be some time before this reactor becomes a factor in Iran's proliferation calculus.

The Iranian centrifuge program reportedly benefited from Pakistani help in the early 1990s (and perhaps more recently) and North Korean help in the late 1990s, and appears to have made steady progress.[10] Iran is currently building a uranium conversion facility at Esfahan to produce uranium hexafluoride feed-stock for its centrifuge program; Iranian officials claim that the plant is nearly ready to start operation. Moreover, a February 2003 IAEA visit revealed that Iran is producing gas centrifuges. (If it tested these using uranium hexafluoride gas before commencing mass production—and it seems implausible that it would not have done so—it may have already broken its NPT commitments.) A visit to a facility at Natanz found a small pilot cascade of 160 centrifuges and parts for 1,000 more, in a facility large enough to accommodate 50,000 centrifuges. The discovery of Natanz has raised questions about the possible existence of clandestine centrifuge cascades elsewhere in Iran.

More recently, the National Council for Resistance—the Iranian opposition group that first revealed the existence of nuclear facilities at Arak and Natanz in August 2002—has claimed that such a pilot plant is located at Kalahdouz (about 14km west of Tehran) and that Iran is building a fuel-fabrication facility at Ardekan (about 30km northwest of Yazd, in central Iran)—presumably to service the fuel requirements of the Bushehr reactor.[11]

In sum, Iran appears well on the way to attaining all of the elements needed to produce large quantities of fissile material by either the plutonium or uranium-enrichment routes. Assuming all goes right for Iran, it could produce its first nuclear weapon within three or four years. The window of opportunity for effective preventive action may well be better measured in months than in years.

North Korea: An Alternative Source of Fissile Material?

Over the past 2 decades, Iran has emerged as the premier customer for North Korean arms, missiles, and, more recently, nuclear technology. Were North Korea to reprocess its declared stock of spent fuel (it appears to have started doing so already), it could separate enough plutonium within a matter of months for five to six nuclear weapons. Pyongyang might then opt to export some of that plutonium. Were North Korea to continue its uranium enrichment program, resume operation of its existing reactor, and complete work on two unfinished reactors, it could be producing enough fissile material within 5 years for up to 50 nuclear weapons per year.[12] Based on its record, there is reason to believe that Pyongyang might be willing to sell fissile material and weapon design data to proliferators in the Middle East and elsewhere. Thus, North Korea offers an alternative, nonindigenous route for the acquisition of fissile material by Iran.

THE CHALLENGES OF PREVENTION

Preventive action cannot stop a determined proliferator as far along as is Iran, though it could substantially delay Iran's nuclear progress. The principal goal of U.S. action would be to delay Iran's nuclear program long enough to allow for the possible emergence of new leadership in Tehran willing to either eschew nuclear weapons, freeze its nuclear program short of the production of fissile material, or act responsibly, should it acquire nuclear weapons.

Intelligence Challenges.

The United States could pay a high price for preventive action, including an anti-American nationalist backlash in Iran, damage to its international standing, and the death of U.S. citizens targeted by Iranian retaliation. Accordingly, U.S. decisionmakers will have to feel reasonably confident that preventive action will significantly delay Iran's acquisition of its first nuclear weapon by a number of years, before they could countenance such a course of action. Simply imposing human or material costs or causing modest delays will—under most circumstances—not likely be considered a sufficiently large payoff to justify the possible risks and costs involved.

Such a cost/benefit calculus will translate to exacting requirements for detailed, accurate, and complete intelligence regarding Iran's nuclear program. Here, the U.S. track record is not particularly encouraging; for years, Iraq, North Korea, and most recently Iran, successfully hid large parts of their nuclear programs from the United States. Significant intelligence gaps concerning Iran's nuclear program may remain. The fact, however, that sensitive information about Iran's nuclear program is finding its way to expatriate Iranian opposition groups indicates that there may be "leakers" in the program who might be willing to provide sensitive information to foreign intelligence services. The possibility that the United States could obtain actionable intelligence regarding Iran's nuclear program should not be ruled out.

Technical Challenges.

The technical processes related to fissile material production create both vulnerabilities and challenges. Plutonium programs may be vulnerable to interdiction due to their reliance on large reactors that produce significant signatures—though it may be possible to locate a plutonium production reactor underground to reduce prospects for detection and destruction.[13] Destroying the reactor at Bushehr or the one planned for Arak might set back Iran's plutonium program several years, provided Iran is not building or operating a clandestine plutonium production reactor elsewhere.

While it would be preferable to target these prior to start-up to avoid exposing civilians downwind to fallout, there may be ways to disrupt operations or destroy the reactors after start-up without releasing radioactive material into the environment and creating a downwind hazard.

Centrifuge programs pose a more complex set of challenges. A large number of workshops and factories may be involved in producing and assembling centrifuges, and they can be widely dispersed and easily hidden. Centrifuge cascades have relatively low electrical power requirements (a tell-tale signature of other enrichment technologies), and can be housed in small, dispersed, nondescript facilities which would be difficult to detect by means of remote sensors, as well as in huge plants—such as the one at Natanz.[14] If preventive action is to have a long-term impact, both centrifuge component production and gas centrifuge enrichment facilities would have to be destroyed, which may not be practically possible. The uranium conversion plant under construction at Esfahan is also a likely target. Destroying it could set back Iran's centrifuge program several years—provided Iran does not possess a pilot plant or duplicate facility elsewhere.

Political Challenges.

There seems to be broad support across political factions in Iran for the government's efforts to acquire nuclear weapons.[15] Thus, should the United States act preventively, it must do so in a way that ensures that such action does not poison the reservoir of pro-American goodwill among young Iranians or derail the movement for political reform, thereby complicating efforts to encourage political change and improve U.S.-Iranian relations. In political terms, overt U.S. military action would entail the greatest risk. For this reason, the United States might first consider other options, such as preventive action by allies, or covert action on its own.

OPTIONS FOR PREVENTIVE ACTION: ALLIED, COVERT, OR OVERT?

Allied (Israeli) Military Action.

Other than Israel, few, if any, U.S. allies would be willing or able to carry out such an operation. However, Iran's leaders (and many others in Iran and elsewhere) would tend to see an American hand behind an Israeli military operation, and Iran might be tempted to strike back in ways that would harm both Israel and the United States (e.g., by encouraging Palestinian or al-Qaida terrorism against Israeli or American targets, or goading the Lebanese Hizballah—with its thousands of katyusha rockets in southern Lebanon—to heat up the border with Israel). Israel, however, might be willing to accept these risks in order to deal with a perceived existential threat.

Covert U.S. Action.

Covert action would probably be the most politically expedient way for the United States to disrupt Iran's nuclear program. It might include one or more of the following measures, including:

- harassment or murder of key Iranian scientists or technicians;

- introduction of fatal design flaws into critical reactor, centrifuge, or weapons components during their production, to ensure catastrophic failure during use;

- disruption or interdiction of key technology or material transfers through sabotage or covert military actions on land, in the air, or at sea;

- sabotage of critical facilities by U.S. intelligence assets, including third country nationals or Iranian agents with access to key facilities;

121

- introduction of destructive viruses into Iranian computer systems controlling the production of components or the operation of facilities;

- damage or destruction of critical facilities through sabotage or direct action by U.S. special forces.

Some of these actions might have only a modest effect on Iran's nuclear effort; others might have a significant impact. Covert action could, however, reduce the risks of a political backlash and retaliation—since it might not be possible for Iranian authorities to determine, for instance, whether the death of a scientist was due to natural or unnatural causes, or whether damage to a critical facility was due to an industrial accident or sabotage.

For covert action to succeed, the United States would have to disrupt both Iran's plutonium and uranium-enrichment programs. This might require a sustained covert campaign entailing various actions—the assassination of key personnel, the recruitment of agents or saboteurs at key facilities, the subversion of critical computer networks, direct action operations against critical facilities, etc. Any one of these actions would be difficult enough to pull off; conducting a sustained campaign in which the United States maintained plausible deniability would be even harder. For this reason, covert action may have a role to play, but is unlikely to have a broad, long-term impact on Iran's nuclear program.[16]

Overt U.S. Action.

Overt military action (e.g., cruise missile and/or air strikes) may offer the best hope for success. For political and operational security reasons, however, the United States would probably avoid staging from facilities in friendly Arab states in the region. (And most Arab states would probably prefer not to aid or abet such an operation, to avoid becoming a target for Iranian retaliation.) U.S. decisionmakers would probably prefer to go it alone, rather than approach regional partners with requests for access, basing, or overflight privileges that would likely yield only marginal military benefits, while possibly compromising the operation and straining relations with important friends and allies.

Such a mission is likely to rely on naval platforms capable of launching Tomahawk land-attack cruise missiles (TLAMS) and strike aircraft against targets in southern and central Iran, while Air Force B-52s and B-2 stealth bombers operating from the continental United States would likely be tasked to strike targets deep in Iran (e.g., near Tehran). Range would not be a problem, and providing they achieve surprise, U.S. forces would stand a good chance of avoiding losses at the hands of Iranian air defenses. Nearly all fixed wing fighter aircraft in the U.S. Naval and Air Force inventory can deliver precision munitions, and the United States has a number of conventional penetrator munitions (such as the GBU-28 laser-guided bomb and the AGM-86D Conventional Air-Launched Cruise Missile Block III) for use against hardened and/or buried facilities. (The Natanz centrifuge facility will reportedly be hardened and buried—protected by several meters of reinforced concrete and buried some 75 feet underground when completed.)[17] There are, however, significant challenges associated with the targeting of hardened, buried facilities.[18]

Overt action, however, is politically problematic. It could prompt an anti-American backlash among formerly friendly Iranians, strengthen the hand of hard-liners, and prompt the regime to retaliate against U.S. interests in the Gulf or elsewhere. For this reason, should overt military action be deemed necessary, Washington would be wise to make a serious effort to mitigate a possible backlash by explaining that its actions derived from a desire to prevent nuclear weapons from falling into the hands of the hard-liners who are loathed by many Iranians for their involvement in repression at home and terrorism abroad. This is a concern that many Iranians might understand—if not share. And through verbal and written warnings, military demonstrations, preventive arrests of Iranian agents, and other measures, the United States should take steps to deter and/or disrupt Iranian attempts to retaliate.

IRAN'S RETALIATORY CAPACITY

Should it choose to retaliate, Iran has several options: it could disrupt oil shipments from the Persian Gulf; attack U.S. Naval assets in the region; or engage in subversion and terrorism against U.S. allies and interests.

Iran could disrupt oil exports and shipping in the Gulf. According to a recently published U.S. defense intelligence assessment, "Iran's navy . . . could stem the flow of oil from the Gulf for brief periods by employing a layered force of diesel-powered KILO submarines, missile patrol boats, naval mines, and sea and shore-based anti-ship cruise missiles."[19] It is unclear, however, what Iranian policy objective would be served by this course of action: such a step would likely invite reprisals against Iran's oil production infrastructure and exports via the Strait of Hormuz (which accounts for about 85 percent of Iran's foreign exchange earnings), causing grave harm to Iran's economy, which is the clerical regime's "Achilles' heel." This is an option of last resort for Iran, to be used only if denied the use of the strait, or if other vital interests were threatened.

Likewise, Iran could attack U.S. Naval assets in the Gulf, and in a surprise attack, it might succeed in inflicting painful losses on elements of the 5th Fleet (the Naval equivalent of a "sucker punch"). There can, however, be little doubt that the U.S. riposte would cripple or destroy Iran's navy. This would likewise be a risky course of action for Iran.

Iran's capacity for terror and subversion remains one of Tehran's few levers in the event of a confrontation with the United States, since—barring the use of chemical or biological weapons—it otherwise lacks the ability to challenge the United States on anything near equal terms. In response to U.S. prevention, Iran might sponsor terrorism in Kuwait, Bahrain, Qatar, the UAE, and Oman—all of which host important U.S. military facilities—to sow fear among the Arab Gulf states and cause them to curb U.S. access to military facilities in the Gulf. And thanks to its ties to the Lebanese Hizballah (considered by U.S. officials as "the A-Team of terrorism") and, more recently, its provision of safe haven and assistance to al-Qaida, it has the means to launch a bloody terrorist campaign against U.S. interests in several continents, and in the United States itself.

Though neither Iran nor Hizballah are known to have directly targeted U.S. personnel or interests since the 1996 Khobar Towers bombing, Iran is keeping its options open: Iranian agents surveil U.S. personnel and installations from time to time, and Hizballah retains a significant presence and support infrastructure in the United States that could be used to mount terrorist attacks on the United States.[20] Moreover, U.S. officials recently claimed that al-Qaida officials in Iran were involved in the planning for the May 2003 bombings of three residential compounds in Riyadh, Saudi Arabia, that killed 25 (not including the nine bombers).[21] Thanks to its ties to Hizballah and al-Qaida, as well as its own intelligence assets, Iran could inspire or initiate attacks on U.S. interests in the Middle East, Europe, South America, and in the United States, were it to decide to do so.

CONCLUSIONS

For a variety of reasons, the Israeli raid on Osiraq was a unique case, characterized by conditions that are unlikely to be replicated again elsewhere. Preventive action by the United States against Iran's nuclear program today would have to contend with intelligence, military-technical, and political challenges more daunting than those faced by Israel in 1991.

Successful U.S. prevention would require exceptionally complete intelligence; near flawless military execution; and deft post-strike diplomacy to mitigate an anti-American nationalist backlash, deter retaliation, and, most importantly, ensure that military action does not poison pro-American sentiment or derail the movement for political change in Iran. The complex, daunting, and somewhat contradictory nature of these challenges (e.g., successful prevention could harm short-term prospects for political change and complicate long-term prospects for rapprochement with a new Iran) only underscores the importance of exhausting diplomatic options before giving serious consideration to military action.

Washington, moreover, must supplement these efforts with a serious push to halt North Korea's nuclear program and to prevent North Korea from emerging as a nuclear supplier to Iran, lest North Korea obtain the means to undo the nonproliferation efforts of the international community in Iran.

Nonetheless, preventive action must remain "on the table" as an option, both as a spur to diplomacy by the international community, and out of a recognition that there might arise certain circumstances in the future in which preventive action might become a viable option: should the United States obtain an intelligence windfall regarding Iran's nuclear program that provides it with a complete and detailed picture of the program; should sabotage/covert action become possible as a result of the recruitment of well-placed agents; or should Iran be found responsible for encouraging or commissioning an act of anti-U.S. terrorism that results in significant loss of U.S. life. Under such circumstances, the United States might be inclined to hit Iran's nuclear infrastructure, as part of a broader retaliatory action against terrorist-related facilities in Iran.

ENDNOTES - CHAPTER 7

1. For more details, see Major General David Ivri, "The Attack on the Iraqi Nuclear Reactor: June 1981," in *The War Against Terror* (Hebrew), Tel Aviv: Revivim, 1988, pp. 31-35.

2. The raid, however, failed to eliminate Iraq's pool of scientific expertise, which was rechanneled into efforts to enrich uranium after the Osiraq raid. It also failed to destroy the highly enriched uranium (HEU) reactor fuel that Iraq later hoped to use in its crash program to build a nuclear weapon after it invaded Kuwait in 1990.

3. It should be noted that Iran knows about the vulnerability of nuclear reactors to air attack from direct experience. In September 1980, in the opening days of the Iran-Iraq War, it unsuccessfully attacked Iraq's Osiraq reactor, and subsequently sustained several successful Iraqi attacks on the Bushehr nuclear power plant in 1985 and 1987.

4. *MidEast Mirror*, January 24, 1991, p. 27; Khidhir Hamza, *Saddam's Bombmaker*, New York: Scribner, 2000, pp. 129-130.

5. For more on the implications of a nuclear Iran, see Michael Eisenstadt, "Living with a Nuclear Iran?" *Survival*, Vol. 41, No. 3, Autumn 1999, pp. 124-148; and Kori N. Schake and Judith S. Yaphe, *The Strategic Implications of a Nuclear-Armed Iran*, Washington, DC: National Defense University, Institute for National Strategic Studies, 2001, McNair Paper No. 64.

6. Presumably, this will be contingent on Tehran agreeing to Moscow's conditions for the transfer of the fuel, which are that Iran will: 1) return spent fuel

to Russia for reprocessing, and 2) sign an additional protocol with the IAEA that will give the latter more effective and intrusive means to monitor Iran's nuclear activities.

7. J. Carson Mark, "Reactor Grade Plutonium's Explosive Properties,", Washington, DC: Nuclear Control Institute, August 1990, 6 pp; Department of Energy Factsheet, "Additional Information Concerning Underground Nuclear Weapon Test of Reactor-Grade Plutonium," at *http://ccnr.org/plute_bomb.html*; Harmon W. Hubbard, "Plutonium from Light Water Reactors as Nuclear Weapon Material," April 2003, at *http://www.npec-web.org/projects/hubbard.pdf.*

8. Director General of the IAEA, *Implementation of the NPT Safeguards Agreement in the Islamic Republic of Iran*, GOV/2003/40, June 6, 2003.

9. Mark Hibbs, "AEOI President Told IAEA Last Week Iran Aims to Construct CANDU PHWRs," *Nuclear Fuel*, May 12, 2003, p. 19.

10. Mark Hibbs, "U.S. Concluded by Early 1990s Iran Bought Centrifuge Know-How," *Nuclear Fuel*, February 3, 2003, p. 3; Mark Hibbs, "Iran Obtained Enrichment Know-How from Pakistan, Intelligence Says," *Nucleonics Week*, January 16, 2003, pp. 1, 12; Mark Hibbs, "Pakistan Believed Design Data Source for Centrifuges to Be Built by Iran," *Nuclear Fuel*, January 20, 2003, pp. 1, 14-16; Douglas Frantz, "Iran Closes in on Ability to Build a Nuclear Bomb," *Los Angeles Times*, August 4, 2003, p. A1.

11. AP, "Iran Sites Linked to Weapons," *The Washington Post*, July 9, 2003, p. A23.

12. Nonproliferation Policy Education Center, "Beyond the Agreed Framework: The DPRK's Projected Atomic Bomb Making Capabilities, 2002-09," December 3, 2002, at *www.npec-web.org/projects/fissile2.htm.*

13. It is worth noting that after the destruction of Osiraq, Iraq investigated the possibility of building a nuclear power plant underground—as a protective measure—and Belgian, French, Finnish, Italian, and Soviet companies were asked to assess the viability of such a project. Iraq allegedly abandoned this approach in 1983 after determining that the costs of going underground were "astronomical." S/26333, "Consolidated Report on the Twentieth and Twenty-First IAEA On-Site Inspections in Iraq Under Security Council Resolution 687, 1991)," August 20, 1993, p. 14. Iraq, however, apparently approached China shortly thereafter regarding the purchase of an above-ground nuclear power plant. According to a declassified U.S. Army document, principle considerations relating to site selection for such a reactor included—not surprisingly— "defensibility . . . from possible attacks" and "ability to camouflage from satellites." Michael Knapik, "U.S. Document Says China Studied Building Iraq a Power Reactor," *Nucleonics Week*, July 4, 1991.

14. On the challenges of detecting clandestine nuclear facilities and activities by technical means, see Anthony Fainberg, *Strengthening IAEA Safeguards: Lessons from Iraq*, Center for International Security and Arms Control, Stanford University, April 1993, pp. 20-41.

15. Karl Vick, "Iranians Assert Right to Nuclear Weapons: Issue Unites Conservatives, Reformers," *The Washington Post*, March 11, 2003, p. A16.

16. Here, it is worth noting that Israel is believed to have undertaken a series of covert operations against Iraq's nuclear program prior to the strike on Osiraq. These actions included the destruction of the Osiraq reactor's core by saboteurs as it awaited shipment from the French port of La Seine-sur-Mer near Toulon in April 1979, and the murder in Europe of an Egyptian-born scientist and several Iraqi scientists associated with the nuclear program the following year. Ultimately, covert action did not obviate the need for overt military action to take out the Osiraq reactor.

17. David Albright and Corey Hinderstein, "Iran: Furor Over Fuel," *Bulletin of the Atomic Scientists*, May/June 2003, Vol. 59, No. 3, pp. 12-15, at *http://www.thebulletin.org/issues/2003/mj03/mj03albright.html*.

18. See, for instance: Clifford Beal, Mark Hewish, and Leland Ness, "Hard Target Attack: Forging a Better Hammer," *International Defense Review*, Vol. 29, July 1996, pp. 32-38; Lieutenant Colonel Eric M. Sepp, *Deeply Buried Facilities: Implications for Military Operations*, Air War College Center for Strategy and Technology Occasional Paper No. 14, May 2000, at *http://www.au.af.mil/au/awc/awcgate/cst/csat14.pdf*.

19. Prepared testimony on the "Global Threat" by Vice Admiral Lowell E. Jacoby, USN, Director, Defense Intelligence Agency, before the Senate Select Committee on Intelligence, February 11, 2003, and the Senate Armed Services Committee, February 12, 2003.

20. Statement of Robert S. Mueller III, Director, Federal Bureau of Investigation, before the U.S. Senate Select Committee on Intelligence, February 11, 2003, at: *www.usembassy.it/file2003_02/alia/A3021103.htm*.

21. Dana Priest and Susan Schmidt, "Al-Qaida Figure Tied to Riyadh Blasts; U.S. Officials Say Leader is in Iran with Other Terrorists," *The Washington Post*, May 18, 2003, p. A1.

ABOUT THE AUTHORS

GENEIVE ABDO has reported from numerous Islamic countries for a decade. She is currently the religion writer of the *Chicago Tribune*. Before that, she worked for the Boston Globe and was the correspondent in Iran for *The Guardian* and a frequent contributor to *The Economist* and the *International Herald Tribune*. She is the author of *No God but God: Egypt and the Triumph of Islam* (Oxford University Press, 2000) and most recently, with Jonathan Lyons, of *Answering Only to God: Faith and Freedom in Twenty-First-Century Iran* (New York: Henry Holt Company, 2003).

PATRICK CLAWSON is deputy director of the Washington Institute for Near East Policy and senior editor of *Middle East Quarterly*. He has published numerous scholarly articles on the Middle East in *Foreign Affairs, International Economy, Oxford Bulletin of Economics and Statistics* and *Middle East Journal*. Also, he has published opinion articles in the *New York Times, Wall Street Journal,* and *Washington Post*. Mr. Clawson was co-convenor of the Presidential Study Group organized by The Washington Institute, which published its recommendations to the new Bush administration in the form of a monograph, *Navigating Through Turbulence: America and the Middle East in a New Century* (The Washington Institute, 2001). His most recent authored and edited works include: *How to Build a New Iraq after Saddam*, editor (The Washington Institute, 2003) and *The Last Arab-Israeli Battlefield? Implications of an Israeli Withdrawal from Lebanon*, co-editor (The Washington Institute, 2000).

MICHAEL EISENSTADT is a senior fellow at The Washington Institute. He is a specialist in Persian Gulf and Arab-Israeli security affairs and has published on U.S. strategy in the Middle East, regional security, nonconventional weapons proliferation in the Near East and Southwest Asia, and the armed forces of Iraq, Iran, Syria, Israel, and the Palestinian Authority. His recent publications include *U.S. Policy in Post-Saddam Iraq: Lessons from the British Experience, 1914-1948*, co-edited with Eric Mathewson (The Washington Institute, 2003), *The Last Arab-Israeli Battlefield? Implications of an Israeli Withdrawal*

129

from Lebanon, co-edited with Patrick Clawson (The Washington Institute, 2000). Mr. Eisenstadt is a reserve officer in the U.S. Army. He served in 1991 in Operation Provide Comfort, and more recently at the United States Central Command (USCENTCOM), on the Joint Staff, and in the Office of the Secretary of Defense during Operation ENDURING FREEDOM and Operation IRAQI FREEDOM.

VICTOR GILINSKY is an independent energy consultant and former Nuclear Regulatory Commissioner under Presidents Ford, Carter, and Reagan. He has been active on proliferation issues for many years, going back to his early work at RAND in Santa Monica, California. In 1971 he moved to the Atomic Energy Commission in Washington, DC, where he was Assistant Director for Policy and Program Review. From 1973 to 1975, he was head of the RAND Physical Sciences Department. From 1975 to 1984, he served on the Nuclear Regulatory Commission, having been appointed by President Gerald Ford and reappointed by President Jimmy Carter. During his NRC tenure, Dr. Gilinsky was heavily involved in nuclear-export issues. In 1982 he received Caltech's Distinguished Alumnus Award. He has a Ph.D. in physics from the California Institute of Technology.

GEOFFREY KEMP is the Director of Regional Strategic Programs at the Nixon Center. He served in the White House during the first Reagan administration and was Special Assistant to the President for National Security Affairs and Senior Director for Near East and South Asian Affairs on the National Security Council Staff. Prior to his current position, Dr. Kemp was a Senior Associate at the Carnegie Endowment for International Peace where he was Director of the Middle East Arms Control Project. In the 1970s he worked in the Defense Department in the Policy Planning and Program Analysis and Evaluation Offices and made major contributions to studies on U.S. security policy and options for Southwest Asia. In 1976, while working for the Senate Committee on Foreign Relations, Dr. Kemp prepared a widely publicized report on U.S. Military Sales to Iran. His most recent publication is "Stopping the Iranian Bomb" which appeared in the Summer 2003 edition of *The National Interest.* Dr.

Kemp received his Ph.D. in political science at M.I.T., and his M.A. and B.A. degrees from Oxford University.

ABBAS WILLIAM SAMII is the senior regional analyst for Southwest Asia at Radio Free Europe/Radio Liberty, where he prepares the weekly *Iran Report*, examining politics, terrorism, military affairs, economics, and social developments. He also covers Iraq and Afghanistan. Dr. Samii's publications include "The Security Relationship Between Lebanon And Pre-Revolutionary Iran," in *Distant Relations: Iran and Lebanon in the Last 500 Years*, Houchang Chehabi and Hassan Mniemnieh, eds. (I. B. Tauris, 2003), and "The Internal Struggle Over Iran's Future," in *The Region at the Center of the World: Crises and Quandaries in the Contemporary Persian Gulf*, Barry Rubin, ed. (London: Frank Cass, 2002). His work has appeared in *Middle East Journal, Middle East Policy, The Weekly Standard*, and *Wall Street Journal Europe*. Dr. Samii received his Ph.D. from the University of Cambridge and was a Fulbright Scholar.

S. ROB SOBHANI is the President of Caspian Energy Consulting. He consults with various agencies of the U.S. Government and members of the U.S. Congress on American foreign policy as well as with private organizations on developing and implementing strategies for development in the Middle East and Caspian Sea region. He serves as an adjunct professor at Georgetown University. Dr. Sobhani has previously worked for the U.S. Agency for International Development and for former Congresswoman Connie Morella (R-MD). He is a regular contributor to national print media on U.S. domestic and foreign policy issues, and a frequent commentator on U.S. and international television and radio networks. Dr. Sobhani received his Ph.D. in political economy from Georgetown University.

HENRY SOKOLSKI is the Executive Director of the Nonproliferation Policy Education Center, a Washington-based nonprofit organization founded in 1994 to promote a better understanding of strategic weapons proliferation issues for academics, policy makers, and the media. He served from 1989 to 1993 as Deputy for Nonproliferation Policy in the Office of the Secretary of Defense and earlier in the

Office of Net Assessment and as a legislative military aide in the U.S. Senate. Mr. Sokolski has authored and edited a number of works on proliferation related issues including, *Best of Intentions: America's Campaign Against Strategic Weapons Proliferation* (Westport, CT: Praeger, 2001).